DRIVEN

About the Author

Susie Wolff is a former professional racing driver and one of the most respected women in motorsport. She began her career in karting with a dream of one day making it to Formula One. After racing at the highest levels across Europe, she made history in 2014 by becoming the first woman in over two decades to take part in a Formula One race weekend.

After hanging up her helmet, Susie brought the same drive to the business side of the sport, leading a Formula E team from the back of the grid to World Championship contenders. In 2023, she became Managing Director of F1 Academy – an all-female series backed by F1 to develop the next generation of female talent and prove that motorsport is no longer just a man's world.

Susie has been widely recognised for breaking down barriers and was awarded an MBE for her contribution to women in sport in 2017.

DRIVEN

Susie Wolff

Afterword by Toto Wolff

**HODDER &
STOUGHTON**

First published in Great Britain in 2025 by Hodder & Stoughton Limited
An Hachette UK company

The authorised representative in the EEA is Hachette Ireland, 8 Castlecourt
Centre, Dublin 15, D15 XTP3, Ireland (email: info@hbgi.ie)

1

A CIP catalogue record for this title is available from the British Library

Hardback ISBN 9781399748858
Trade Paperback ISBN 9781399748865
ebook ISBN 9781399748872

Typeset in Minion Pro by Hewer Text UK Ltd, Edinburgh
Printed and bound in Great Britain by Clays Ltd, Elcograf S.p.A.

Hodder & Stoughton policy is to use papers that are natural, renewable
and recyclable products and made from wood grown in sustainable
forests. The logging and manufacturing processes are expected to
conform to the environmental regulations of the country of origin.

Hodder & Stoughton Limited
Carmelite House
50 Victoria Embankment
London EC4Y 0DZ

www.hodder.co.uk

To my wonderful family –
the constant through every chapter,
the calm in every storm,
the loudest cheer in the crowd.

For the belief, the laughter, the sacrifices.
For letting me chase something bigger and never asking me
to be less.

Thank you – for everything.

1

'M beginning to wake up, but waking isn't what I want.

I force myself to stop the thoughts – cutting them before they take root. *Sleep*.

I feel myself waking again. This time, my eyes open. In the darkness I see my husband, peaceful, his chest rising in a steady rhythm. I daren't look at the clock. Don't need its numbers to tell me what I already know. I need more rest. Come on, Susie, *sleep*.

Jolting wide awake, the faint blue glow of early morning seeps through the curtain. Finally I can get out of bed. Nerves tight, I draw one curtain to the side – puddles glint in the dim light. Above, the sky stretches out, heavy with grey clouds. A fizz of anxiety hits my stomach. It's wet, but it's not raining. That's a positive. I can't control the weather. I can only focus on getting everything else right.

I turn around and head for the bathroom. It's time to get ready. The waiting is over. A goal I have been working towards nearly my whole life is about to become a reality. Today I'm going to drive a Formula One car for the first time.

I pull the front of my hair into a plait and then back into a ponytail. I test it once, twice, tugging gently to ensure there's no chance of it slipping, no stray hair to irritate or distract me. With my hair pulled back, I catch a glimpse of my neck. It's always been big. Too big for my frame. I usually wear my hair down or a scarf to hide my hulk-like trapeziums, but I would still get the inevitable question: what do you do to get a neck like that? The answer had been years of racing, but for the last four months, it had also been a machine developed by Michael Schumacher. Strapped in, my head was tethered to a network of weights. A brutal rehearsal for the G-forces lying in wait.

Left.

Right.

Forward.

Back.

Every time, I fight it – neck locked, muscles screaming – resist, resist, resist as the pain sears down my neck and spreads through my shoulders. It never got easy, but it got easier. And now the day I've been fighting for is here, and it is now.

My team kit is hung up in the cupboard, everything in perfect order, each piece steamed and pressed. The shirt, the trousers, even the socks – arranged deliberately, in the exact order I'll put them on. There's a rhythm to this, a quiet, methodical process that steadies me. Each detail, no matter how small, offers a kind of comfort, a semblance of control.

The one thing I can't control is the weather.

Driving down the motorway to Silverstone, I see the clouds begin to break, streaks of blue slicing through the grey. I will the sun to fight harder, to burn through and dry the wet patches. Closer to the track, the light shifts – the grey fading into the orange glow of morning.

As I enter the paddock, five big Williams F1 trucks are neatly lined up outside the garage. There is a hive of activity, mechanics, in the distinctive Williams F1 team kit, wheel in sets of tyres wrapped in heat blankets. I head straight to the engineering truck to put my race suit on. A makeshift curtain has been set up, a small, thoughtful gesture to give me a sliver of privacy to change. I can picture the conversation that must have taken place – a discussion on how to accommodate a female driver, something they've never dealt with before. The quiet awkwardness of moments like this isn't new to me – it has been a constant undercurrent throughout my career.

One last time, I inspect the label on my racing suit to ensure it is the exact same one I have worn while moulding the seat at the factory. Every detail – the pedals, head height, body weight – has been calibrated to the decimal point in that suit. Preparation is a mentality – and the power is in the details.

As 9 a.m. approaches, I step into the meeting room and take a seat next to my engineer, Dom. We met four months ago during my first simulator session at the factory. Quiet, introverted, impossible to read – he never lets on if I am doing well or not. The others are already in place, heads down, fully focused: the performance engineer, the power unit engineer, the data analyst, the aerodynamicist, the tyre specialist, the simulator technician and the chief technical officer.

The briefing starts, and each detail is summarised: an installation lap followed by two ten-lap runs. For now, there is too much standing water on the track, so we will wait. As expected, the first run will be on wet tyres. Dom gives me a sympathetic glance – we both know what that means. All those hours spent in the simulator, endlessly lapping Silverstone in dry conditions, now seem futile. Every braking point and gear shift I have memorised, every cornering speed etched into muscle memory, will be irrelevant. I'll be stepping into the unknown with only my gut feeling to rely on. And above all else, although no one dares to say it, is the overriding thought – I hope she doesn't crash.

When I step into the garage the sweet smell of high-octane racing fuel hangs in the air. I have always loved that smell. The car has already been fired up. A modern F1 car demands seven engineers running hot oil through the engine for forty minutes just to get it to a working temperature. Outside, the media has started to gather, their numbers growing. Cameras and journalists hover at the edges. It's part of the game – it always has been. I am a curiosity, something new and untried. I don't resent them, and I don't love them. They're just there, another piece of the puzzle. Anticipation has reached fever pitch. All eyes are on me. The question hangs heavy in the air: can a girl handle a modern F1 car? Today, there will be a story – it is inevitable. Success, or I'm finished. That's how it works. Simple. Brutal.

Dom approaches; they want me to do an installation lap and get a measure of how much standing water there is and whether a run on wet tyres is even possible. At last, the waiting, the talking, the endless observing are over. It is time to leave the small talk and scrutiny behind.

My earplugs, custom-moulded to fit perfectly, bring a welcome, muffled silence as I press them into place. I savour the stillness, a fleeting moment of calm. From now on, it will be just me and Dom – me in the car and him at the monitor. He will see what I can feel, deciphering the multicoloured lines of telemetry: the G-forces, the speeds, the cornering precision, every slide and slip of the car etched into data. Data which will reveal my every move, good or bad, to be pored over and judged.

Before I climb in, a mechanic wipes the sole of each foot, ensuring they are bone dry to avoid any risk of slipping on the pedals. This is something I always insist on as part of my process – no dirt or water can be allowed to compromise my grip on the pedals. Once I am in the car, he fastens the seat-belts. He knows I'll ask for them to be pulled tighter; I always have to insist, as no mechanic ever tightens them enough because they're worried about hurting me. I tug down on the belts – I want to feel welded to the chassis itself.

He clicks the steering wheel in place, its dense cluster of knobs and buttons in the centre. I had taken it home, spending hours obsessively practising on it, drilling every button, dial and knob into my memory so that when a command comes over the radio, I don't need to think twice. It feels like solving a Rubik's Cube – colourful and deceptively complex.

Pink left: neutral.

Pink right: reverse.

Yellow left: drink system.

Yellow right: pit limiter.

Red: kill switch.

White: brake balance.

Light blue: oil circulation.

Orange: radio.

Knobs for differential adjustment, KERS, engine, torque maps . . .

Each flick, twist and press has had to become second nature.

I look up to a sea of cameras, all trained on me, ready to capture the moment. To the right, Sir Frank Williams watching on. Dom spins his finger to give the signal to go; everyone covers their ears as the V8 engine roars to life, the thunderous growl reverberating through the garage and my body. I make myself conscious of the vibrations pulsing through the steering wheel. I am ready. I have gone through this moment so often in my head that although it is the first time, it feels familiar.

I slowly release the clutch paddle and feed in the throttle, searching for the bite point, that delicate threshold where the engine begins to transfer power. Too much throttle and I'll spin the wheels; too little, and I'll stall. I ease the car forward out of the garage and into the pit lane. Well, thank goodness – the girl hasn't stalled it.

As I emerge onto the track, I steadily climb through the gears. Almost immediately, I am on the long straight. As I brake hard, the car begins to shift and squirm beneath me. Exiting the corner, the rear end snaps out sharply, and my hands jerk the steering wheel instinctively, wrestling the car back into line. The rain-soaked asphalt means that, with every corner, I will need to gauge the limits, feeling my way through the variations in grip.

The puddles haven't gone but the standing water has dissipated enough for it to be safe. I get the command over the radio to return to the pits. As I stop, the car is instantly surrounded by a swarm of mechanics and pushed back into the garage. I report no issues. Dom confirms the car will be checked over, and we'll immediately start the first run. I anchor my thoughts on the present moment, refusing to let them stray. I visualise with clarity exactly what I have to do.

Out on track for my first run, I accelerate through the gears until I reach full speed. The G-forces tug my helmet upwards with such ferocity that I suddenly think, *Did I do my helmet up tight enough?* I am acutely aware of the fine line between being fast and slipping off the edge. It feels like a dance – uncertain at first, every move on the edge. But with each lap, my instincts kick in, sharper and steadier. The nerves fade, replaced by something stronger: a determination that whispers, *This is where you're meant to be. You've got this.*

Laps completed, I pull into the pit lane, and the mechanics wheel me back into the garage. Dom appears by the car, and though he doesn't smile, the relief is written all over his face – and the faces of the mechanics. I haven't crashed. When I'd first walked into the simulator room at Williams, I'd felt the quiet scepticism. No harsh words, no hostile gestures, but unmistakable all the same – I was a token gesture, a nod to diversity. I had learned that the way to silence it was simple:

keep my head down, work hard and perform. Because performance is power. Now, as I look around the garage, the energy has shifted. It is different from this morning – lighter, sharper. Without a doubt, Dom and every single person there are with me, willing me to succeed.

I am out of the car, leaning on the pit wall, watching the track dry in the sun. Thin trails of steam rise where the water was evaporating, and I can see it – a narrow, dry racing line starting to form. It isn't much yet, but it is there. Dom walks up beside me, quiet for a moment as we both watch the track. I don't wait for him to ask.

I think we can go out on slicks, I say, still looking at that faint line.

He glances at me, then back at the track, and nods.

The final session is upon me, and this time it isn't just about keeping the car on the track – it is about being fast. It is one thing to avoid spinning off in the wet, but now I have to prove I can be quick. Theories, simulations, hours spent memorising every braking point and cornering speed – they've all led to this moment. Now, theory will meet practice.

Hurtling through Woodcote and Stowe I feel my lungs pushed up against my ribcage. One G is the force of your own body weight – imagine five times that force ricocheting your head, like the fastest of rollercoasters taking the tightest turns, over and over again. The strain on my neck through the high-speed corners and under braking is unrelenting but the pain also brings familiarity. I have grown to get comfortable when it gets uncomfortable.

I hammer down the throttle. The barriers blur past as the engine screams. Copse looms, the fastest corner at Silverstone, it's all or nothing as downforce sucks the car to the track. Lift even a fraction, and you'll be slow. Then it's into the gut punch of Maggotts and Becketts, where the car snaps left, right, and left again. The G-forces hit like a freight train. Then on to the long Hangar Straight where I reach in excess of 300kph.

There is absolutely nothing else occupying my thoughts and senses except each intricate detail. The precise calculations of where I can brake later, where I can carry more speed. Speed and competitiveness have always been at the core of who I am, a natural drive to push boundaries and chase the stopwatch. In that moment, I am laser focused, consumed by the need to nail the perfect lap, to extract every fraction of time I can.

Dom's familiar voice crackles in my ear: *Last lap, back to the pits.*

Was that it? Already?

The car is pushed back into the garage for the final time, and suddenly the exhaustion hits. My body feels heavy, my neck and shoulders throbbing from the relentless strain. But endorphins surge, chasing away the ache. Relief washes over me – I have shown what I can do, left nothing on the table. It is over, but I'm not ready to climb out just yet. The weight of the moment settles in. This might be my last time in an F1 car.

I let the calm seep in, savouring these final seconds before the whirlwind resumes and the inevitable rounds of media interviews start. I've always preferred the *doing* to the *talking*.

As I step out of the car and walk to the back of the garage, a few mechanics pat me on the back. Is it because they don't have a damaged car to repair or because the girl has done well? Either way, it is something.

I take off my helmet and feel an arm around my shoulder. Glancing to my left, I see Toto.

It was good, he says.

Being Austrian, he never wastes words. Direct, to the point and never gushing. Before I can even reply, he is gone. I barely have a moment to process before someone tells me it is time to face the media. Williams said it was a one-off – just twenty-five laps. But I don't believe in 'just'. When life cracks the door open, you don't wait for permission – you charge through and grab your chance. My chance is now.

2

CAN still see the path, winding through the thick bracken that blanketed the hills behind my house. My PW50, a 49cc kids' bike, was struggling to keep pace with Mum and my brother on their bigger bikes up ahead. My helmet jangled on my small shoulders because my neck was too weak to absorb the bumps. We stopped at a clearing, and there it was – the steepest path we had encountered yet, stretching endlessly into the sky, or so it seemed to my six-year-old eyes.

Mum's voice broke through the rumble of the engine.

Full throttle, don't stop! For her, more throttle was the answer to most things in life. She couldn't stand staying still – she was happiest in motion, always needing something to do, preferably something physical. She had to grow up fast. Her dad, my grandfather, was paralysed in a diving accident when she was twelve, struck by the bends and confined to a wheelchair. Life changed instantly for them, but it never stopped him from being larger than life, dragging the family along for the ride. I'd seen an old black-and-white photo of him launching his BSA bike over a crest during the Scottish Six Days Trial, which he nearly won. His son, my Uncle Mike, would follow in his footsteps. Gramps was one of those classic English action men who seemed to do it all: paratrooper, works BSA rider and, later, a commercial diver. After his accident, he continued to fly microlight aircraft well into his fifties, before being banned by my grandmother, Mo, after breaking his ankle during a crash landing. He made up for what he lacked in displays of affection with his unshakeable can-do and never-complain attitude. Anytime we grumbled, Mum would ask if we'd ever heard Gramps complain. Of course, we hadn't.

Go, go, go! Mum shouted as my brother's engine revved, and he shot up the hill.

Typical. Being over a year older, he always went first and always set the bar high. My heart was racing. Mum turned to me.

Straight up. No stopping.

Well, if David could do it, I could do it. I had seen my mum racing bikes with my dad. She bought her first bike from Dad's motorcycle shop when she was young, and that was it – they hit it off, and before long, they were racing quad bikes together, living for the thrill. When my brother and I came along, we became part of the adventure. I remember being packed between quad bikes, bouncing along on old duvets and cushions on our way to motocross races. It all felt so normal, seeing Mum racing with the men, seeing her afterwards, red-faced and covered head to toe in mud, swapping race stories with Dad and their mates.

I leaned forward, lifted my foot off the ground and twisted the throttle. The bike jerked ahead, and suddenly, I wasn't in control – I was just along for the ride. The faster it went, the more I was pushed back, which made me twist the throttle even harder. I was barely hanging on, nearly tossed from the seat. The bike bucked beneath me, kicking up dirt and grass. I strained with all my might to keep my eyes locked on the brow of the hill as it came clearly into view. Then, before I knew it, the bike launched over the crest – I was at the top. David was already there, waiting by his motorbike. He smiled and gave me the thumbs up. Even though I was the little sister, often slowing him down and no doubt frequently annoying, he always treated me as an equal. He wanted me to succeed, to keep up with him – we were in it together.

I felt a surge of adrenaline. It was as if every nerve lit up at once, carrying a flood of energy that I came to love. That moment wired me for more. I'd chase that feeling again and again.

Mum arrived right after.

Well done, she said, as if she'd expected nothing less.

Before I could dwell on the lack of effusive praise I thought I'd earned, we were off again, looking for the next hill – one that now seemed much easier. The brilliance of my mum's expectation was that we at least give it a go. We had unconditional love but not universal praise – that had to be earned.

I grew up in Oban, a small town on the West Coast of Scotland, where tourism had gradually replaced fishing as the backbone of the local economy. Drawn by the opportunities it offered, my parents both found their separate ways to Oban, nestled by the sea and surrounded by rugged hills.

My mother and her brother, Mike, had grown up in Derbyshire where Gramps ran a motorbike shop that exclusively sold British bikes – BSA and Triumph. He was a proud loyalist to these iconic brands, but his refusal to embrace the rise of Japanese manufacturers such as Honda and Yamaha eventually made his business unsustainable. Searching for a fresh start, he moved the family to Oban, inspired by his trips to Scotland and the dream of turning his other hobby, diving, into a professional career. After Gramps's diving accident, Mo, stoic as ever, stepped in as the glue that held the family together.

My dad, on the other hand, was born and raised in Glasgow. His father, my grandpa, worked as an engineer for Rolls-Royce, becoming the youngest foreman on the shop floor. Both he and my grandma had high hopes for their only son. They lived frugally, sacrificing so they could send him to a private school, believing education would open the doors to a better life. My dad tried to make good on their dreams – he started studying pharmacy, then switched to optometry, diligently trying to meet their expectations. But deep down, he knew it wasn't for him. He dropped out, packed up his tools and became a mechanic.

He loved motorbikes, and racing quickly became his passion. One day, he opened a map and noticed that a region as vast as Argyll had no bike dealerships. That was all the motivation he needed. He drove to Oban, asked a local rider where he'd bought his motorbike, and when the answer came back as Glasgow, he knew he'd found his opportunity. He set up shop, sleeping there until the business gained traction. In time, Granny and Grandpa joined him in Oban.

My mum met my dad when she went to buy her first motorbike, no doubt encouraged by Gramps. She bought the bike, but by all accounts, Dad didn't give her any discount. They became friends, and with their shared love of motorbikes they were soon going to my dad's race meetings together. By then, he had started taking road racing more seriously, competing in events like the Isle of Man TT, the fastest and most dangerous road race in the world. Their friendship grew through frequent squash games and eventually became a romance, marked by holding hands in the back of a van on the way to a race. True to form, my mum, never one to beat around the bush, gave my dad an ultimatum nine months later while they were on holiday in St Lucia.

Are we going to do something about this, or just keep bubbling along? she asked.

My dad, ever the romantic, replied, *I'm 99 per cent sure you're the one.*

It wasn't until happy hour cocktails loosened him up a few hours later that he turned to her and said, *Sal, I think we can give this a go.*

The next morning, with sore heads, my mum reminded him of his words, half expecting him to have forgotten. But he hadn't. Soon after, they were engaged.

Within a year of getting married, my mum was pregnant. Parenthood didn't dampen their enthusiasm for racing; in fact, when my dad got a new racing bike, my mum insisted on taking it for a lap around Knockhill, the only racetrack in Scotland – five months pregnant. She had to push her belly to the side of the fuel tank to make it work. After my brother was born, my mum decided she wanted her children as close in age as possible. Sixteen months later, I joined the family.

We grew up in a house near Ganavan, a white sandy beach whose name means 'white sand' in Gaelic. For me, it was a magical place, a giant playground where my brother and I could run wild. Behind our house was Battleship Hill, a steep and rugged hill that we spent hours exploring, making dens out of whatever we could find, or racing each other to the top. The only rule was simple: be home before the streetlights flickered on. It was a different time – when kids ran free and parents trusted the dusk to call us home. My two best friends were Heidi and Judy; we were inseparable all through primary school.

By that time, Mum and Grandma had opened their clothes shop, and with both parents working, David and I started spending more time during the week with our grandparents. We loved it. We'd head up to Mo and Gramps's campsite where we had free rein of the kids' play park. True to form, Gramps had built a playground that would have given any health and safety inspector a nervous twitch – underground tunnels that got smaller and smaller, a zip line and some formidable climbing obstacles. Eventually, most of it had to come down because it was deemed too risky, but for us, it was paradise.

On alternate days, we'd be taken up to Grandma and Grandpa's. There was always soup, whatever Grandpa had made that week, served at the kitchen table like clockwork followed by whatever delight Grandma had baked.

David and I moved as a little team, though I usually had to do the negotiating. I'd charm the bus driver into holding on just a moment longer while David sprinted out the front door, school jumper half on, tie askew, hair everywhere. Always late. Always grinning.

Around this time, my parents started selling jet skis at the motorbike shop, and soon we had a family jet ski rental business on the beach with all the extra equipment for watersports. On sunny days, David and I were in charge of fitting customers with life jackets, taking payments and timing their rides. We were always doing something – my mum's aversion to sitting still meant there was never a dull moment. On weekends, if the weather was good, we'd be out on the sea from morning till night.

The Gulf Stream passed by Oban, keeping the climate from being as harsh as Siberia, but it was far from tropical – the cold water still stung. To help, Mum and Dad had custom wetsuits made for us by a local company. What thrilled me most wasn't the practicality but the fact that I got to choose the colours. At last, I could be like my prized Ocean Snorkel Barbie, with her pink and light blue wetsuit. Just like her, I adored anything pink.

I loved Barbie – she could be anything. Rollerblade Barbie, Ski Fun Barbie, Scuba Diver Barbie, Business Barbie. I'd spend hours creating my own worlds, where nothing stopped her. She'd drive her pink convertible, her pink van or her pink speedboat. She was unapologetically girly but could do it all.

I'd lay out a blue towel to mimic the ocean, setting up my Wet 'n Wild Ocean Friends speedboat, driven by Ken, of course, while Ski Fun Barbie water-skied behind.

So, when it was my turn to try water skiing, I was determined to channel Ski Fun Barbie. My dad, on the jet ski, ever confident in my abilities, hit the throttle and I shot forward – straight into a faceplant. But I didn't let go. Instead, I was dragged underwater, saltwater forcing its way into my eyes until my hands finally gave out. Spluttering and coughing, I bobbed back to the surface, thoroughly un-Ski Fun Barbie. I'd watched my brother gripping the rope behind the jet ski, crashing but then managing to get up, and we were all cheering from the beach.

Back on shore, I reasoned with Dad, *Okay, I'll try three times, and that's it.*

All right, Toots, he said, using his pet name for me, *but get up on the first try, and I'll buy you that Barbie you won't stop talking about.*

Cowgirl Barbie! Suddenly, the goal was clear, this wasn't just about water skiing. This was about getting Cowgirl Barbie. I ran to my brother, wide-eyed and desperate. Sitting me down on the ground, he patiently demonstrated the technique. Arms straight. Back upright. And knees tucked into my chest. And the most important part: when you feel the rope pulling, you push against the water with your skis, straighten your legs and lean back. He went over it one last time before we both jumped in off the jetty. Dad, already perched on the jet ski, flung the rope towards me.

Okay, Toots, get ready!

My brother offered his last bit of advice: *Only losers let go.*

The rope went taut, yanking me out of the water, and suddenly I was up. My skis skittered across the surface, my arms bouncing, legs wobbling and body bent forward, graceless but upright. But I wasn't letting go. I hung on until I hit a small wave and went crashing down into the water. Again, very un-Ski Fun Barbie – but I didn't care. Cowgirl Barbie was mine.

Being cold is a consistent childhood memory. Sunbathing wasn't our thing. Holidays were action-packed; the idea of lying on a beach was alien to my mum. At Christmas, we always went to the mountains in France – Mum and Dad were avid skiers, and they had us on the slopes almost as soon as we could walk. By the time we were two or three, they had us toddling around in the snow, set on turning us into little racers. We joined the École de Ski in France, part of the Young Ski Club, where each trip brought a new badge and a sense of progress. Every single Christmas, we'd be in France with a group of other families. Mum and Dad's passion shaped our holidays, and they were determined to get us racing down the runs as a family, no matter the conditions. But sometimes, that mindset led us a step too far.

One such moment came when I attempted to ski down a difficult slope. Mum and Dad, standing at the top, encouraged me to go for it. Following Dad, with Mum behind us, I went, but I didn't stop. There were no turns, no control – just sheer, reckless speed. I passed Dad, and he quickly realised I wasn't in control and, in a state of panic, skied after me. The only way to stop me was to collide with me. His quick thinking probably saved me from something much worse further down the hill, but the crash itself was spectacularly bad.

The next thing I remember was waking up in an ambulance, Mum's calm but insistent voice beside me: *Don't go to sleep, keep your eyes open.* The paramedics were concerned about a head injury, and that moment, I think, was when Mum and Dad truly became scared. I ended up in the hospital with a suspected fractured skull, and the whole ordeal kept me there for two days. I was back on the slopes the next day, but our ski schedule eased up for the rest of that trip. It was back to full attack the next year, though.

Part of Mum and Dad's reasoning was that whenever something bad happened, it was important not to dwell on it. They didn't want it to become a psychological barrier for us. So, the next year, I was back on the slopes with maximum effort, under the understanding that accidents happen. For my parents, it was a lesson learned – next time, they made sure I was sandwiched between them on the slope. But they weren't scared of risk; they were determined to get me back out there and not let fear take hold. You pick yourself up and you keep going.

Motorbikes were a constant in our family. My dad had encouraged my mum to take up quad racing, insisting she was part of the action and not watching from the sidelines. Before long, we became part of a travelling group of riders from Oban, making long journeys from our remote town to beach races across the UK. Although we travelled with other families, ours was unique – my mum was the only mum racing. That was entirely down to my dad, who believed that anything he could do, Mum could do too.

At the age of three, I remember waking up on Christmas Day to find two cards, one for my older brother and one for me. Each had a ribbon attached, his blue and mine yellow, and Mum and Dad told us to follow them. Excitedly we followed the ribbons around the house until they led us out of the front door and on the drive were two mini three-wheelers with 50cc engines, each with our names on the side.

Soon, I was obsessed with motorbikes. As a family, we would go and watch MotoGP at legendary circuits like Assen in Holland, Donington and Silverstone. My bedroom walls were a shrine to the sport, plastered with posters of my heroes – Kevin Schwantz, Mick Doohan and Wayne Rainey. My homage to all things racing, and I couldn't get enough of it.

In stark contrast to motorbikes was the business my mum and Grandma started – a dress shop called Bennetts, specialising in wedding outfits and elegant women's attire. Mum would come down the stairs dressed for work, often in a sharp skirt suit and heels, ready for the day ahead. She looked so glamorous in her Jacques Vert suit, bright lipstick and heels – a striking contrast to how she was at the track, dressed in overalls. I marvelled at how effortlessly she could pull off both looks.

On Saturdays, having just turned eight, I'd help out in the shop, dusting the display cabinets filled with jewellery, hats and shoes. When customers came in looking for something special, I was in charge of making the tea and coffee, watching as Mum and Grandma thoughtfully considered which designer and colour palette would suit them best. The curtain of the dressing room would pull back to reveal a stunning outfit, and the customer, now more poised and confident, seemed transformed from the person who had first walked through the door. The tailor would be called to make the final touches, adjusting arm lengths and hems to perfection. Princess Diana's mother, Frances Shand Kydd, was a regular customer, and Mum took quiet pride in ensuring she found just the right outfit for her frequent visits down to England.

On certain occasions, Mum and Grandma took me out of school to join them on trips down to Glasgow to buy stock for the following season. We'd get up early and I'd dress in my best outfit, not wanting to look out of place next to both of them. Each designer's showroom was filled with glamorous dresses and gowns for consideration, the saleswomen eagerly showing off the new styles of the season. Bennetts gave me a front-row seat to the power of clothing and style – the way they could elevate not just an appearance but a person's whole demeanour.

My first real taste of competition came not with motorbikes but with swimming. I wasn't built for it – one of the youngest in the Scottish school year, born in December, and always the smallest in the class. My parents even arranged a doctor's visit to check if something was stunting my growth. Turns out, I was just a late developer. Still, my brother and I raced through swimming grades, setting our sights on the Oban Otters Squad. It was invitation-only, training three times a week under Callum, the ex-policeman coach whose booming voice could cut through the water like a knife. 'The Squad' strutted poolside with their sleek goggles and water bottles, and I was desperate to be one of them.

When the tryout date was announced, it felt like everything hinged on that moment. Both my brother and I would compete, with the top eight swimmers earning a spot. I could see it already: the yellow-and-black swimsuit, the matching cap, the cool tracksuit for competitions. Long before manifestation became a buzzword, I'd daydream what it felt like to succeed.

On the day, we lined up at the pool's edge, split into groups, and given drills to showcase speed and technique. I focused on moving cleanly through the water, glancing at the coach out of the corner of my eye every third stroke. He'd occasionally pull a swimmer aside for feedback, but not me. Was that a good sign? I couldn't tell. When we finally climbed out, shivering and red-faced, Callum stood before us, clipboard in hand. Names were called, one by one. My brother's name came and I cheered under my breath, whispering, 'Yes!' Then my best friend Heidi's. I hugged her quickly as she moved forward. Four names left. Then three. I willed my name to be called. But it wasn't. I stood frozen. I hadn't made the team. The chosen eight congratulated each other, and then my brother and Heidi rushed over to me with words of encouragement that felt like pity. I hated it. Anger bubbled up. Staring at the coach, I thought, *You just made a mistake. Big mistake. Huge.*

While my brother and Heidi moved on to train with the squad, I wasn't about to sulk. The local gala was coming up and I was determined not to be left behind. Every training session became a battle to prove myself. I was small, my stroke was messy and I lacked natural grace, but I made up for it with raw effort.

The day of the gala arrived and I couldn't wait to get onto the starting blocks. No one saw me as a threat – the other girls were taller, stronger with their long, graceful strokes. But I'm a scrapper, and so when the gun fired, I gave everything I had. My stroke was frantic, a splashing mess, while the others glided with control. I didn't care. My muscles burned and my lungs screamed, but I refused to stop. In the final metres, I couldn't see anyone in my eyeline. When I hit the wall, I realised I'd won. The exhaustion hit, I tried to climb out but I slipped back. I tried again but I had nothing left. Eventually, Callum pulled me from the water without a word.

My grandma, watching from the stands, summed it up perfectly: *It wasn't pretty, but it got the job done.*

At training the following week, Callum said without any fanfare, *You'll be training with the squad from now on, Susie.* And that was it. What had started as anger from being overlooked had turned into energy, a tap into a deep reserve within. I learned to embrace it. Channel it.

Between school and all of our sporting pursuits, life was action-packed but Dad had just turned forty and was determined to reignite his road racing days. Perhaps in the midst of a midlife crisis, he bought a road racing bike. Once again, as a family, we were off, following him through various race meetings. Knockhill became our usual haunt. While Dad tore around the circuit, David and I kept busy with our little motorbike, a Yamaha PW 80cc. We'd take turns racing along the outskirts of the track, weaving through the paddock like we belonged in the thick of it.

My pride and joy were my pink and aqua motocross boots, paired with a pink jacket. While I spent a lot of my time doing tomboyish things, I loved pink. My Barbie dolls were always in the back of the van for downtime. As I waited for the bike to come back, David rode over.

Get on the back, he said. He'd spotted some older kids to race against. There was no way I was sitting this one out. I jumped on and clung to him tightly as we roared off. Up ahead, a couple of older kids were on a sleek 125cc water-cooled bike.

My competitive streak flared. *Go faster!* I yelled, urging David to catch up.

We trailed behind until a steep downhill appeared.

Flat out! I shouted, and David obliged. Against all odds, that tiny 80cc bike, with me still clinging on for dear life, picked up enough speed to blast past the 125.

The thrill was glorious – right up until it wasn't. A sharp corner came out of nowhere. David lost control and we crashed spectacularly, tumbling off as the bike skidded away. Cuts and bruises everywhere, but my first thought wasn't the pain. It was the scratches on our precious bike . . . and my boots! Furious, I turned on David, bruised and bleeding, blaming him entirely for the scratches on the bike and swearing I'd never ride with him again.

Mum, watching the chaos unfold, must have had enough. We couldn't keep tagging along to watch Dad race while wreaking havoc on the sidelines. David and I always begged for £5 to drive the local kart track at Knockhill, and that gave Dad an idea. Maybe it was time to trade bikes for something we could all do together: karting.

3

As I got close to turning nine, Dad sold his road bikes and bought us two second-hand karts. Made by a company called Swiss Hutless, they had a striking red frame and a lot of rust, but they were ours. I remember being completely in awe of them – they felt so sleek and fast compared to the hire go-karts we'd been used to. We spent days practising on the small circuit at Knockhill. When Dad was busy at the motorbike shop, Mum would drive us two hours from Oban, and we'd stay all day, testing, learning and racing each other. On the way home, the lessons continued. Mum would give us racing line tutorials as she drove, demonstrating how to cut corners, hit the apex and guide the steering wheel. She'd explain that every time we tightened the wheel, we scrubbed off speed – so our goal was to straighten out the corners as much as possible. Every time we approached a bend, she'd ask, *How should we tackle this one?*

It was our version of 'I Spy', a game to play in the car, and it was as much a part of our racing education as being out on the track. Eventually the feeling was we had outgrown that small track and it was time to go to a proper kart track and get racing.

Our first-ever race was at Larkhall, a track wedged between a scrapyard and the motorway. It was the premier karting circuit in Scotland, and stepping into that world completely blew our minds. It was only club-level racing, so the first step on the motorsport ladder, but the level of competition was unlike anything we'd imagined. These were families who karted every weekend, their vans and awnings spread throughout the pits like a mini racing village. In contrast, we had arrived with a trailer, everything we needed thrown in the back, looking like complete novices – which, to be fair, we were.

As rookies, my brother and I had to wear black novice plates with our numbers, starting all three heats from the back of the grid, the results of the heats setting the grid for the final. Nothing from our Knockhill practice sessions had prepared us for the blistering speed of these kids. It wasn't long before we were being lapped, and the experience was brutal. The other racers had no qualms about knocking me out of the way as they overtook, their aggression leaving me rattled. Complaining to my dad about the rough treatment earned me a response that's still etched in my memory.

Two options, Toots – put the kart back in the truck, or go back out there, try to go faster, and when they hit you, hit them back twice as hard.

Well, of course I chose the second option. Slowly but surely, during those first few months, racing every second weekend, my brother and I improved.

Part of the reason my dad chose karting was so all four of us could race together. When he mentioned this plan to other karting families, they told him we were mad – there was no way we could manage four karts between us. In a way, they were right. Race meetings were utter pandemonium. On wet days, there were sixteen tyres to change, and when the weather fluctuated, chaos reigned. I remember one time it started raining heavily and my dad sent me out on slicks, tyres designed for the dry conditions with absolutely no grip in the wet, because it simply wasn't possible to change all the tyres in time. In hindsight, it wasn't the worst lesson. British drivers are known for excelling in the wet.

Grandma and Grandpa came along to help as well, offering their support where they could. Mum and Dad's race was often the next one after ours, so they would help collect our karts from parc fermé, a secure area where karts are held, after the race – no mean feat, especially considering Grandpa was battling emphysema at the time. But he wouldn't let that hold him back. Between working on the karts and taking his nebuliser, he was always there, doing whatever he could to help, with Grandma on catering duty. In the chaos, it was a family effort.

I'll never forget the time David and I were in the same race, battling for the lead. From my perspective, I was ahead when he took me out. David, of course, claimed he was up the inside and

I'd turned in on him. We both stuck to our stories, and the van ride home was silent except for the sound of the road. Hours passed before Dad finally said, *Come on, kids, this is ridiculous.* We exchanged glares and stayed stubborn. That was the moment Dad decided we'd never race in the same class again.

After a couple of years racing as a family, my parents made the decision to step things up. It was time for my brother and me to become the focus of the racing. We had demonstrated real promise after a strong showing at the Scottish Championship, and that success spurred us to take the next big step. The decision was made: we would compete in the British Championship. This shift meant all the family's energy and resources were now directed towards supporting my brother and me on this new and more competitive stage.

We thrived as the racing grew more intense and competitive. Karting quickly became our main focus, with dinner conversations dominated by upcoming races. Weekends were no longer spent at home – they were spent at the track. We seized every opportunity to practise and prepare. But it never felt like pressure; it felt like purpose. Karting gave us a shared focus, a channel for our energy, and it brought us closer together as a tight-knit family unit.

Our first trip to England for the opening round of the British Championship was a humbling experience. The trucks were enormous, the awnings stretching endlessly, and professional kart teams dominated the paddock. With our van and trailer, we couldn't help but feel a little out of place. But Dad, as always, remained unflappable. Calm and easygoing, his go-to mechanism was humour – cracking jokes to keep us all laughing.

There were clear favourites on the track and we quickly learned who to watch out for. Helmet designs became our shorthand for spotting the fastest drivers. One name kept cropping up: Lewis Hamilton. His bright yellow helmet made him impossible to miss and his reputation had already taken on a life of its own. He'd started racing at eight, and by ten he'd won his first British Championship. He wasn't just fast – he was a benchmark.

My parents quickly realised that if we were serious about competing at this level, we'd need more support. They were enthusiastic, but also realistic – they knew they needed someone with deeper experience, someone who truly understood the world of racing. Enter Duncan White, our kart supplier and engine tuner, and a fellow Scot. He didn't mince words.

Buddy, it's just not good enough, he'd say, before breaking down exactly what needed fixing. His critiques were blunt but invaluable, and over time, we came to rely on him completely. So much so that my dad asked him to join us at the track every weekend. With Duncan on board, we started thinking about karting on a whole new level.

Suddenly, it wasn't just about driving – it was about settings, tweaks and adjustments we'd never considered before. We experimented with axles that were two or three millimetres different in size to change the flexibility at the back of the kart. We switched to magnesium wheel rims because of how efficiently they managed heat on the tyres. We used rods connecting the chassis to the seat to stiffen the kart, giving it a whole new feel. Duncan pushed us to understand every part of the kart, and he started asking us for detailed technical feedback on how it felt to drive. I learned to describe what I felt – where it understeered, where it was biting too hard – so Duncan could make precise adjustments.

It was an education in what it meant to feel and communicate with an engineer, lessons that would shape everything I did in racing moving forward. Somehow, hearing the tough truths from Duncan was easier than hearing them from my parents. We respected him, trusted him and knew he only wanted us to succeed.

But racing wasn't the only thing I treasured on those weekends. Once the day's sessions wrapped up and the karts were cleaned, the paddock turned into a playground. Barbecues were fired up, kids kicked footballs around and remote-control cars tore through the tarmac. Those long evenings, full of laughter and games, were just as important as the racing. They reminded me that the track wasn't just about competition – it was also about community.

These weekends spent racing felt worlds apart from my classmates' experiences. On Mondays, when I'd hear about their adventures, they seemed alien to me. Likewise, when I'd return from a British Championship, racing against the best, and tell them I'd finished a respectable sixth, their blank expressions made it clear they didn't quite understand what that meant and weren't particularly impressed.

Unlike most of my peers at high school, I was never that interested in boys. I was surrounded by them most of the time. It's not that I didn't get Valentine's cards – there was even a big card tied to two balloons left outside my door once – but my focus was entirely on racing. In hindsight, maybe that focus made me more intriguing. I was racing a lot during that time and threw myself into other sports too. My energy went into competing, not dating.

I was always studious and organised – a bit of a swot. My folders were perfectly arranged, my notes meticulously kept, and I lived by to-do lists. My dad still jokes about finding one where the first item was 'get up'. At least I knew I'd start my day with a sense of achievement. I had no problem spending my evenings studying hard to get good results. My pencil case was always packed and colour-coded, and every evening I'd prepare my school bag and lay out my uniform for the next day. That sense of order and attention to detail extended to every part of my life.

I was well behaved, and often overshadowed by my brother in the year above, who was a bit more wayward. While he stirred things up, I seemed to pass through unscathed. Although we didn't take part in many extracurricular activities, my parents insisted we join the public speaking club. They believed it was important for us to learn how to speak confidently in front of others. We competed in regional debates, and while I didn't think much of it at the time, rehearsing speeches and presenting arguments turned out to be a discipline that would serve me well throughout my life.

By then, although I wasn't yet thinking about a future in motorsport, when it came time to choose a language at school, I asked my dad what he thought, as I wasn't particularly interested in either French or German. He told me that some of the most iconic car manufacturers were based in Germany, so the choice became clear. German was a hard language, and I most definitely wasn't naturally gifted, but my teacher, Mr Stewart, was patient. He acknowledged my effort, even if my grasp of grammar wasn't perfect. My colour-coded, immaculate notes might not have made me fluent, but they showed I was trying.

I relished being at the forefront – whether it was winning competitions or representing the school. One day, a surprise assembly was called and we were told that game show scouts were looking for contestants. The show? *Fun House* on ITV – the dream for every kid. The audition, they explained, would include rounds of activities: impressions and group challenges. My mind raced.

My brother, the budding filmmaker, often insisted on filming me doing impressions or dances on our parents' camcorder. I wracked my brain. I could do a solid Boycie from *Only Fools and Horses*.

When my name was called, I got up, heart pounding. I grabbed a felt-tip pen from my pencil case and pretended it was a cigar. Strutting forward, I launched into my act, imagining the casting director was Del Boy and I was laying into him with a full-on Boycie impression. I was way out of my comfort zone, but the laughter in the room gave confirmation it had gone down well.

Then came the group challenge: a balloon-popping race. We were split into teams and tasked with bursting as many balloons as possible. Watching the first runners struggle, I knew I needed to think outside the box. An idea struck me – the metal clip on my watch's strap. Pop, pop, pop. I tore through the balloons, clearing nearly all of them before the other team had managed three. Subtle? Probably not. But the casting director seemed to appreciate my creative problem-solving. Sure enough, I made it onto the show.

Travelling to Glasgow with my teacher and classmate, Lorn, was a big deal. It was my first time away from family, and I would be sharing a room with a girl from the opposing team. Her name was Becky; I remember her being kind, and we were both very excited to be on the show, struggling to sleep at night. But despite the fun we had together, we both wanted to win. I was in the red team, and they were yellow.

Part of the show involved a go-kart race, and on the first day, we were brought to a warehouse to practise. For everyone, it was their first time in a kart, and the instructor carefully explained how to use the throttle and brake. I listened, nodding along, scared I'd be disqualified if they knew I raced. When it was my turn, I even asked, *Which one's the brake again?* During the practice laps, I deliberately drove cautiously, blending in with the group.

On the morning of filming, the reality of being on *Fun House* hit me. The iconic set, the colourful outfits and the games – it was all exactly as I'd imagined. Then Pat Sharp, the host, was introduced to us. He was affable and warm, but as soon as the cameras started rolling, he transformed into this hyper, over-the-top personality I recognised from TV. Pat informed us that we were competing for the best prize of the series – a trip to New York. Now, it was time for the two teams to face off, battling for the chance to run the gauntlet of the Fun House and claim victory. It was Red vs Yellow.

The games began. The first was a race where we slipped through slime and grabbed the rope to climb a slippery slope with giant-sized rubber cheese, lettuce and a sausage to make a hot dog. My thoughts of a strong start were quickly put to rest. I got slime in my eye, I slipped off the slope and tumbled behind Becky. The Honey Bee challenge was even worse. Lorn failed to get any honey in the pots or answer the question, 'What is a female bee called?' (It's Queen Bee.)

By the end of day one, we hadn't won a thing. Back in our hotel room, Becky was already commiserating with me, promising to send me a postcard from New York. I thought, *Not so quick, Becky – it isn't over yet.*

The next day brought the go-kart race. This was my chance. The race was structured so one teammate would drive twice and the other once. Lorn and I strategised – I would go twice in the go-karts and he would do the Fun House twice, if we got that far. The go-kart felt like a toy compared to what I was used to, but the second I hit the throttle, I was pulling away from the Yellows. The aim was to grab as many tokens as possible, but I wasn't about to settle for one at a time. At every station, I scooped up handfuls – two, three, maybe even four at once – never taking my foot off the throttle. I flew around the course, hand darting out to grab more and more, the tokens piling up as I raced back to the finish line.

After the race, Pat, still full of energy, started counting the tokens, dropping them into clear plastic tubes to see who had the most. Pat and the studio audience realised we had won before I did. I looked over at Becky, stunned. It would be me sending her the postcard.

The final challenge was the Fun House itself. We had to collect tickets, each representing a prize. The studio buzzed with energy as we scrambled through the maze, grabbing tickets and hitting buzzers. Then came the ultimate question for the grand prize: 'What are the three colours in the British, American and French flags?' Lorn hesitated, glancing at me. 'Blue, red, white,' I said boldly. The buzzer sounded, and we'd won!

The grand prize – a trip to New York – felt surreal. My parents later converted it into a ski holiday so the whole family could share in the experience. True to our family's ethos: we did everything together.

As I turned twelve, life started to revolve more and more around karting. I had given up swimming and skiing to focus on racing; there was no time for anything else. After school, David and I would head to Dad's workshop to clean the karts, while Dad rebuilt the engines and Mum tackled the mountain of laundry so we were ready to race the following weekend. In my typically organised way, I started making folders to keep track of all the settings we'd tried at different tracks, neatly sectioned so we could better understand setups and improve with every outing. Our playroom shelf was soon stripped of cuddly toys and transformed into a display for our growing collection of trophies.

By then, Dad had invested in a bigger truck with a living compartment in the front and a workshop in the back. There were cold nights in the truck, where we would curl up in bed to stay warm, going to bed fully dressed with race suits under our pillows to keep them from freezing. Mornings started with steaming cups of tea and bacon butties, savoured as the frost clung to the windows. It became our home away from home as we travelled to tracks as far afield as Yeovil in south-west England, sometimes driving twelve hours straight through the night.

We'd often arrive just in time for Friday practice, spend the weekend racing and then face the long journey back on Sunday night. By Monday morning, we'd be rolling into Oban just before the morning bell, changing into our school uniforms in the truck, hopping out and heading straight to class. Mum and Dad, exhausted from driving through the night while we slept, bore the brunt of the effort. We'd innocently comment, *That didn't take too long.* For us, it was all part of the adventure; for them, it was a way to keep the family together.

At the British Championship, the competition was a step up. It was the best of British and you had to qualify in order to take part. It was contested over twelve race weekends, with the winner going on to compete with the highly coveted race number 1. On tough weekends when results didn't go our way, which was more often the case at the beginning, the drive home could feel endless. I hated that feeling. It would take days before the knot in my stomach would slowly release and be forgotten about.

My way of coping with bitter disappointment was simple: I worked harder. Every Monday after school, I'd head straight into Dad's workshop, cleaning my kart and mentally preparing for the next race. Since my swimming days, I had learned to lean on my imagination – daydreaming the scenarios and outcomes I wanted, turning them over in my mind until they felt real. Dad, ever supportive, always reminded us that bad weekends built character – a lesson I took to heart, though I often thought, *Well, I've definitely got enough character now.*

There was no pressure to race – the drive came from within. We wanted to be out there, pushing ourselves to improve. After a good weekend, Dad's quiet pride said it all. Sometimes he'd get emotional after a race, and in those moments, it felt like we were repaying Mum and Dad for all their effort and sacrifice. On the way home, we'd stop at one of our favourite restaurants, analysing the weekend as a family and already planning for the next.

I was often the only girl racing, but it never even crossed my mind to think of it that way. Out on the track, with my helmet on, it wasn't about gender – it was about performance. It was about being faster, smarter, better. My parents never once made a fuss over the fact that I was a girl doing something most girls didn't. For them, it didn't matter if I was their daughter or their son. Karting was just something we did as a family, something we loved. And for me, that's all it was – a thrilling, shared hobby. Until it wasn't.

One weekend, a few months before my fourteenth birthday, with no racing planned, Duncan, who was now a permanent fixture in our team, called and asked if we fancied coming down to Donington to watch Formula Three. *One of my old drivers is competing,* he said. F3? I didn't even know what that was, and honestly, I wasn't all that interested in watching other people race.

I found out that Formula Three is the third tier of racing, just two steps below Formula One, and a crucial proving ground for any young driver with F1 ambitions. F3 cars resemble smaller versions of an F1 car and it's often where top teams scout for emerging talent.

When we arrived, I was floored. The sheer scale of it – the track, the trucks, the cars – it was like stepping into a completely different universe. Everything felt enormous. Serious. Professional. We walked into one of the garages and I barely said a word. I was overwhelmed. The team uniforms were spotless, the tools and equipment lined up in perfect order. There was an electric buzz in the air, a tension that was almost tangible. It wasn't just clean, it was clinical. And yet, it wasn't cold. It felt like purpose and precision. Like everything had a place, a reason.

As the race drew closer, we made our way up to a balcony overlooking the track. I watched as the cars roared out of the pit lane and onto the grid, their engines screaming with power. I'd seen MotoGP before, seen the best riders in the world. But this? This was different.

That day, a young British driver named Jenson Button won. But it wasn't the race or the winner that hooked me. It was the realisation, quiet at first but growing louder with every lap, that I could do this. I could race at this level. The jigsaw pieces that I hadn't even known were missing started clicking into place. Racing wasn't just something I loved. It was something I could do for a living, not just a hobby.

On the seven-hour drive home, I pelted Duncan with questions. What made a good F3 driver? How could I progress up the ladder from karting to F3? What did it take to get from there to F1? I listened to every answer, storing each nugget of information like treasure. By the time we pulled into our driveway, my mind was made up.

I climbed the stairs to my bedroom, tore down every MotoGP poster on the walls and sat on my bed, staring at the blank space. I was going to be a racing driver. I was going to make it to Formula One.

4

IT'S 1998, and I'm sixteen years old. Pay-as-you-go mobile phones are just starting to take hold, but selfies and social media are still a decade away. I had no real concept of what I looked like – there wasn't even a mirror in my bedroom. Mum had bought me a Clinique makeup set, a subtle nudge towards womanhood, but it wasn't something that interested me, so it remained largely unused. Meanwhile, the world outside was being shaped by the rise of lads' mags. Women were being slotted into two stark categories: the ladette, downing pints with the boys, or the scantily dressed male fantasy plastered across the covers of those magazines.

My dad's friend Mario, who ran a pub in Oban, made an offhand comment that stuck with me: he said he was sure I'd get pregnant and end up working in my dad's shop. It hit a nerve. There was already a scandal in my school class with a girl my age getting pregnant, and for some reason it terrified me. The idea of my freedom being taken away, of being trapped in a life expected of me, felt suffocating. In my mind, having a boyfriend was part of that, even though it was becoming the norm at school.

At the school disco, I watched from the sidelines as my classmates coupled up. It wasn't that I didn't want to join in, but Mario's prediction echoed in my mind. It became a warning. I wouldn't let myself go down that road. I would actively reject any advances because they would get in the way of what I really wanted: to stay in control of my life and make it to F1.

I started drifting away from my school friends. Their weekend activities, meeting boys or sneaking into discos underage, felt less and less like they belonged in my world. While their bedroom walls were plastered with posters of Take That and Westlife, mine featured Scottish F1 driver David Coulthard, fist raised in triumph behind the wheel of his McLaren. For me, it wasn't a celebrity crush – it was about something bigger. He symbolised my ambition.

The dynamics began to change at the karting track: we were now racing at the highest level and boys were turning into young men. The atmosphere on and off the track began to change. Gone were the days of casual, childish games. Now, there was a sharpness, an edge, to everything we did. The stakes had been raised, even if none of us could quite articulate why.

Off the track, the conversations started to change too. I began to notice how the boys spoke about girls – their tone shifting, the way they talked about the sisters of other drivers, turning casual observation into something more loaded. I often stood on the edges of those conversations, silent, realising I didn't want to be spoken about like that. All I could do was listen.

One of the sisters, though, had a knack for defusing it. When the boys stared at her, she'd shoot back, *What are you lot looking at? Do I have a telly on my head?* She met their gaze, unfazed. She knew how to handle herself, but it made something click for me.

I started to see the way women were viewed differently – the way the male gaze could reduce a girl to an object, the way reputations were made so quickly, often based on nothing. The double standard was obvious: boys were boys, but girls were judged. It was unfair, it was wrong – but it still shaped me. Quietly, almost without realising, I began to shrink from that kind of attention. I didn't want to be looked at like that. I didn't want to be talked about. Not in that way.

This shift bled into the racing itself. The competition became more intense, more aggressive. It wasn't just about beating lap times anymore; it felt personal. If I passed a boy on the track, it was like flipping a switch. Suddenly, he would dig deeper, find extra speed, fight harder to reclaim his position. I wasn't just another racer – I was a motivator, a benchmark to be beaten. It became clear that being quick wasn't enough. I had to toughen up – find an aggression that didn't come naturally. Every pass I made felt like it carried extra weight, not for me but for the boys too. It didn't help that some dads couldn't resist having a go at their sons when I beat them, saying things like, *I can't believe you let a girl beat you.* You could see the frustration on their faces, and it only made the boys push harder. Those comments were like throwing petrol on a fire.

In a heat of the British Championship at a track near Yeovil called Clay Pigeon Raceway, the aggression on track hit fever pitch. The racing was tight and no one was giving an inch, least of all to me. During the rolling start – a slow lap before crossing the line to begin the race – the driver behind me kept slamming into my kart. He was one of the drivers from a very wealthy family, with a sense of entitlement to match. Each jolt sent a clear message: he wanted to rattle me, to throw me off my game before the race even began – this wasn't just about racing, it was about asserting dominance.

The race began, and we were off. Fighting my way through the pack, I couldn't shake him. He tried to overtake but couldn't pull it off. We were evenly matched, slugging it out for a few laps until he decided he wasn't about to stay stuck behind a girl. At the end of the straight, he launched me off the track and into the tyre wall.

I saw red – a hot wave that blurred everything else. Sweat and tears stung my face as the crushing reality sank in: my chance was gone, obliterated in that instant. There was no way I'd make the final. My mum and dad were upset; I was seething, as I came in last. His move hadn't gone unnoticed and we were both summoned to the Clerk of the Course – motorsport's equivalent of a referee. True to form, my dad insisted I represent myself. We had always been pushed to stand on our own two feet, fight our own battles. No crutch, no parents fighting our corner. I wasn't intimidated. This was on me.

In the small office, it was just me and my nemesis, with his father looming behind him. We were asked to present our versions of the event. I stood there, listening as he spun his story, downplaying the collision and suggesting I'd caused my own misfortune. His father chimed in, backing him up and insinuating it was all my fault. Well, I wasn't having it. I went forensic, detailing exactly where I'd braked, how consistent I'd been each lap, and how unacceptable it was to be taken out just for competing. Standing there, I started to speak up for myself. The stakes shifted. This wasn't about the race. It was about proving that I, a girl, deserved to be there. I wasn't going to be dismissed so easily. Point by point, I laid it all out. The Clerk ruled in my favour. My nemesis was disqualified. Justice, maybe, but my weekend was still ruined.

After that weekend, it dawned on me that the rules of the game had changed. If I was going to survive in this world, I was going to have to change too. The pink suit had become a target, a signal that I was different. I realised they perceived my femininity as a weakness. I ditched the pink and bought a blue-and-white suit with a sparkling silver stripe. The silver, maybe, was the smallest nod to femininity, like a whisper of who I was. But mostly, it was blue. With my helmet on, I could easily be mistaken for a boy. This was more than a change of clothes: it was a metamorphosis. I had to become one of them. Like Barbie, my pink race suit was packed in a storage box and tucked away in the loft.

Almost every weekend, we were racing. Dinner conversations dissected every heat and final from the previous race weekend. While other girls my age were flipping through magazines like *Just 17*, I was reading *Karting Magazine*, poring over the race reports for a mention of my name.

For my personal project at school, I chose the Williams F1 team. In a bold and overly optimistic move, I wrote to every F1 team asking for a summer work experience placement. I was far too young, and the teams were based much too far away, but I did receive one kind reply from Benetton, encouraging me to write back in a few years.

On track, the highlights started stacking up. No standout wins yet, but I'd moved up a class to Formula A, the pinnacle of karting. My competitors were no longer boys but young men. I was still small, but the hard knocks on track were tempering me, toughening my resolve. I wasn't afraid to fight back, to muscle in, just as I'd been muscled out so many times before. Now I was mixing it at the top.

Towards the end of that season, I found myself locked in a battle for fourth position. Nose to tail, lap after lap, I couldn't find a way past. Then, as I approached a tight corner, I hit the brakes – and nothing happened. My kart didn't stop. I flew over the back wheel of the kart ahead, barrel-rolling as the momentum launched me high into the air. I landed with a thud on the track. The race was stopped immediately. Dazed, unable to process what had just happened, I lay motionless as the world around me blurred. An ambulance arrived and I was loaded in.

The brakes had failed. I was okay, but the crash was a serious wake-up call. For all my bravado, I wasn't invincible. From that day on, my mum couldn't bring herself to watch my races. She preferred to walk around the paddock, waiting for the summary when I returned to the truck.

Weeks later, at a round of the British Championship, things started to click. I qualified second. The hard work was finally paying off. As the weekend ended, we gathered around the back of the truck while the last kart was loaded in for the long trip home. My dad and Duncan were deep in conversation before Dad gestured for me to come over. *We think it's time, Toots*, he said. *The European Championship.*

I'd heard tales of racing on the continent: more grip, over 130 entries and the best drivers from every country. Bring it on. Within days, it was arranged – I'd be joining the legendary Peter de Bruijn team for the European Championship. It wouldn't just be our family driving the truck and doing everything ourselves. This was another level. It was a significant expense, but it would replace our family holiday that year, and we were all-in. I didn't know the exact figures, but I understood even then the financial strain it placed on my parents. Duncan was at every race, supporting me tirelessly, and Colin, our family friend, affectionately called Wally, joined us to lend his skills as a mechanic.

Peter de Bruijn was Dutch. He had beaten Ayrton Senna to the World Karting Championship title in 1980 and had since built a powerhouse team, guiding drivers such as Jos Verstappen to European Championship victories. But what intrigued me more was his wife, Lotta Hellberg. Swedish and formidable, she came with a reputation that preceded her. She had finished fourth in the World Karting Championship, an almost unheard-of achievement for a female driver at the time. I'd kept every magazine clipping about her. If she could do it, maybe, just maybe, so could I.

Our first meeting wasn't what I'd envisioned. Lotta didn't exude warmth, and the bond I'd imagined – two women in a male-dominated world – didn't materialise. She barely spoke to me. Peter was far more approachable. Occasionally, I'd catch Lotta watching me from a distance, but most of the time, she was busy running the team. One driver, a notoriously relaxed Finn, often napped in the truck between sessions. As practice approached, Lotta's shouts echoed: *Where's Kimi?!* Eventually, Kimi Räikkönen would saunter out, half-asleep, helmet in hand, and proceed to dominate – infuriatingly effortless, a stark contrast to me. But I was used to working harder – at school, at the kart track. I didn't mind, as long as I managed to achieve what I set my sights on.

After one practice, as I walked back to the awning with my kart, Lotta stopped me. My lap times were starting to show real promise, edging closer to the pace of the top drivers. Things were looking up, but the physical demands at this level were something I had never experienced before. Lotta, though distant, seemed to be paying attention. I'd spot her at the side of the track, stopwatch in hand, silently timing and taking it all in.

How are your ribs out there? she asked.

My ribs were battered. The extra grip on the track punished my body under braking and cornering. My hands blistered, my back ached and bruises spread across my ribs. But I wasn't about to admit any of it.

Fine, I said, keeping my game face on.

Does your rib protector fit properly? she pressed. Of course, it didn't. Rib protectors were designed to cushion your ribs from the pressure of cornering and the jolts of bumpy tracks. Without them, the fibreglass seats could cause hairline fractures from the sheer speed and G-forces, especially through high-speed corners. But they weren't made for female torsos.

Mine, the smallest size, had extra Velcro to tighten it, but it was far from comfortable. The rigid design pushed down on my chest, an awkward fit that never let me forget it wasn't built for my body. I had tried to customise it as much as possible, adding layers and adjustments, but nothing could get around the fact that it simply wasn't made for someone like me. Still, it was better than nothing.

You're tough, she said, her tone softening.

Not always, I replied.

They made one specially for me, she said, inspecting my makeshift version. *It actually fits properly.*

I waited for her to tell me where she got it, or how I could get one, but she didn't. *Great*, I thought, *very helpful.*

The next morning, Lotta was waiting by my kart. *Come with me*, she said. I followed her through the paddock to a van, where a man named Steve Tillett was already waiting for me. Lotta explained he was going to create a custom rib protector – one designed specifically for me. He began moulding the plastic around my ribcage, carefully shaping it to accommodate my chest. Unlike the standard ones, this design curved under my chest instead of flattening it. It wrapped securely around my waist, strengthening me from the bottom up. As he worked, I realised the significance of what she was doing. Lotta, the only female role model I'd ever had in racing, was handing me something that might seem small to others but carried enormous meaning for me. She was giving me my own armour – one female warrior to another. I have that rib protector to this day.

After this, we became closer and she showed me, every race weekend, how to be a woman in a man's world and not lose any of yourself. She never said it out loud: there was never a heart to heart, but what she gave me was even better. She had a suit specially made for me with a single pink lapel on the left-hand side – a subtle nod to my being a girl without making it the focus, bringing pink back into my life in a way that felt right for me. Lotta was tough, battle-hardened and didn't take any nonsense, but was still feminine with long blonde hair. I saw glimpses of who I wanted to become in her, and what it would take to get there. We both respected performance above all else. I wasn't interested in token gestures, but I believed in the sisterhood, and so did she – an unspoken pact that we lift each other up. She showed me how this could be done in a genuine way that wasn't ostentatious or shallow.

I was riding a wave of optimism. But racing has a way of humbling you. Before the final of every European Championship race, there was a flag procession. Every nation's drivers grouped under their flag and paraded around the track to the music of Vangelis's 'Conquest of Paradise'. It didn't matter where you finished; the idea was to stand and represent your country. Mum and Dad encouraged me to go, even though I hadn't made the final on my first attempt. I'd shown some promise, and they felt it was important to take part.

I remember making my way over to the British contingent, where all the boys I'd raced against in the UK were gathered. I took my place waiting for the procession to begin but no one spoke to me, I wasn't included in the conversation. However, it was still a moment of pride – to stand alongside those I'd competed against, representing our country. Then, one driver turned on me. Told me I didn't belong there, that I couldn't walk with them. Was it because I hadn't made the final or because I was a girl? The only girl? I didn't know, but I froze, unsure of what to do, as the weight of his words sank in. Embarrassed and humiliated, I walked back, my face burning with shame. The worst part was explaining to my parents. I realised then, for me, there is nothing worse than being pitied. They felt sorry for me and I hated it.

The European Championship had coincided with my Standard Grade exams, the Scottish equivalent of GCSEs, with one exam scheduled for the Monday after the race. Oban High School arranged for it to be sent to a school teacher in France who lived near the racetrack. Exhausted from the weekend, I went straight back to the hotel to study and the next day arrived at the teacher's house to take the exam. There was no time to dwell; I had to compartmentalise, focusing on the exam ahead. Racing came with a deal: Mum and Dad would sacrifice to get me on track, but my schoolwork had to hold up my end of the bargain. In the end, it paid off – I came out with six As and two Bs.

Rounding off the year was the World Championship, the focal point of my season. One hundred and thirty drivers had qualified, but only thirty would make the final, determined by six heats over two days. Lewis Hamilton, the favourite, raced alongside Nico Rosberg in a powerhouse team. My qualifying position placed me in the top ten for each heat. The first five went well – three top-six finishes and two in the top ten. But my body was wearing down. My muscles ached, my neck and shoulders screamed, and by the morning of the final heat, the pressure was palpable. One more top-ten finish and I'd make the final. I finished seventh. Was it enough?

We waited in the awning, tension thick. Duncan handed me the result sheet. *You're in, buddy. You're in.* Thirtieth place. I had just made it, but I was in. Now, with nothing to lose, it was time to attack.

As expected, Lewis led, but then his engine gave out halfway through. As the laps wore on, the physical toll began to hit me hard. My ribs ached like never before, each corner sending searing pain through my body. It felt like a war of attrition, but I kept counting down the laps, pushing through the agony. Lap by lap, I clawed my way through the field. By the time the chequered flag waved, I had made it up to fifteenth.

As we were packing up, happy with the result and how much ground I had made up in the race, I suddenly heard my name over the loudspeaker: *Susie Stoddart to the podium ceremony.* Confused, I ran to the main stage. First place, second and third trophies were handed out. Then, I was called up – Top Female Driver in the World.

My face burned with embarrassment as I stepped onto the stage in front of all those who had earned their podium places. I wasn't there to be the top female. I was there to try to win but was being singled out as different. I hadn't even registered if there were any other women in the competition; it had never dawned on me to look for them.

Motorsport had always been the one arena where men and women could compete as equals – where gender wasn't supposed to matter. But this award, with its separate category for me, shattered that illusion. It carved out a box I hadn't asked for, underscoring a difference I'd spent my whole karting career trying to erase. I was fighting to prove that talent mattered more than gender, I didn't want special treatment – I wanted a level playing field. I wanted to win. On the same terms as everyone else.

5

STARED at the computer screen in the stuffy IT room at school, answering question after question. The cursor blinked, daring me to make a decision.

Do you prefer working with people, data or things?

Would you rather work indoors or outdoors?

Do you enjoy creative activities like drawing or writing?

Rate how much you enjoy the following subjects: mathematics, history, physical education.

At first, I tried to answer carefully, picturing the life each choice might lead to. But the test dragged on, and eventually, I just clicked through, barely thinking, letting instinct take over.

When I finished, the computer hesitated like it was making some grand decision. Then, the dot-matrix printer sputtered to life, spitting out a sheet of perforated paper. I tore it free and read the word: 'Accountant'. Just one word, one future. I was eighteen, and it felt like my path had already been decided.

With the slip of paper in my hand, I waited outside the career officer's room. He opened the door, glanced at me and motioned me in. I handed him the paper and sat down.

The computer got it wrong, I blurted out.

Well then, he said, leaning back in his chair, *what* do *you want to do?*

I met his gaze and said it as clearly as I could, without hesitation. *I want to be a racing driver.*

He looked at me like I'd just told him I wanted to be an astronaut or a movie star.

That's interesting. He paused. *But what are you going to study?*

My grades were very good, and the expectation was that I would go to university and, like the rest of my friends, it seemed like the only option at that time. After my encounter with the careers officer, that expectation only intensified. Steered towards accounting – because I was good with numbers, organised and liked structure – I chose international business, focusing on the international aspect as it still offered a chance to travel and experience the wider world.

I didn't overthink it – business made sense. I didn't spend time visiting campuses or exploring universities, or thinking about the possibilities they might offer. I got an unconditional offer from Edinburgh University. Just like that, the decision was made.

Meanwhile, on the track, my peers were stepping up from karting to single-seaters – high-performance, open-wheel racing cars. The next step on the ladder was Formula Ford and I knew that was where I needed to be to progress, but the costs were staggering, a massive leap from karting and far beyond what my parents could afford. Still, I had one thing the rich kids didn't – I was a girl, and there weren't many of us. After much discussion, we decided to test a Formula Ford, to see what I was like in the car. Mum and Dad cashed in one of their pension policies to pay for a test at Pembrey Circuit, with a team called Wayne Douglas Racing.

The seating position in a single-seater was worlds apart from karting. You're practically lying back, with limited vision out of the car and just a glimpse of the front tyres. It felt alien, like starting from zero all over again. I didn't know the track, and nothing about the car felt familiar. The first day was rough – seconds off the pace, no rhythm, no connection to the car. I could only imagine what the team must have thought. Here was this girl who had finished fifteenth in the World Championship, and yet I looked completely out of my depth. And I was.

By the end of that first day, one thing was clear: I had a mountain to climb. The car demanded muscles I wasn't used to using, the seating position was awkward, and the lack of downforce in the Formula Ford meant the car moved around unpredictably. It didn't drift exactly, but it felt loose, like it could step out at any moment. That night, I went back and studied the track map, determined to find something, anything, to improve. Everyone says you sleep on it and it gets better. By the next morning, it did. My first run was already quicker than my best from the day before. It wasn't much, but it was progress.

I didn't talk much during those two days. I took everything in – the inputs from Wayne and the team – and focused on finding my way. It wasn't a top team at the time, but Wayne had a reputation as a racer turned team owner, someone who knew how to spot potential. By the second day, I was making strides, enough to show I wasn't a lost cause. I think Wayne saw that too. He knew I didn't have the money to go racing at the level I needed, but he believed in the promise of that progress.

Through Wayne I was introduced to a man named Paul. Paul wasn't a sponsor, but he came from a business background and had a love for racing. He told us he'd worked with other well-known drivers and knew how to navigate the tricky world of motorsport funding. He said he saw potential in me and promised to start looking for the money, to find a way to get me back on track. That meeting, coming after a tough but promising test in the summer, gave me hope, but at least with university, I had covered off a backup plan.

The day came to pack up my room and load everything into the car for the drive to Edinburgh. It wasn't far – just two and a half hours from Oban – but it felt like a world away. I was enthusiastic; as much as university wasn't my priority, I was ready to take a step towards independence, however small. Leaving home meant escaping the inevitability of working in my dad's shop or following the well-trodden path of settling down early. This was my chance, my first real taste of something bigger.

When we arrived at Darroch Court, my university accommodation just off the Royal Mile, I was struck by how modern the building was. I hadn't expected it to feel so new or to be so close to iconic landmarks like Holyrood Park and the Royal Mile itself. For a girl from Oban, Edinburgh still felt like a big city, its history and grandeur slightly overwhelming. But I was ready for it – or so I thought.

I was given my flat number and shown to my room. It was bright and spacious, with a bed, a desk and a wardrobe. The shared kitchen and living room were clean and inviting, and for a moment, I felt positive about the adventure ahead. My parents helped me unpack, bringing in boxes as I tried to take it all in. Then, one of my flatmates arrived.

Sarah bounded into my room, chatty and full of energy. She immediately announced how much fun we'd have and wasted no time pulling me into her plans. That first evening, after my parents left, she dragged me out to buy groceries for the flat. Later, we went shopping, wandering through stores I'd only heard of – French Connection and others I'd never had access to back home. It felt novel, almost exciting, to be exploring a city that seemed so full of possibilities. I walked around Edinburgh in awe, passing the castle and soaking in the feeling of living in a place so steeped in history.

But as the days passed, the differences between Sarah and me became more obvious. She loved going out, meticulously planning her outfits days in advance, talking enthusiastically about the boys in the other flats. I didn't own any 'going-out' clothes, I'd never needed them, and I had no interest in the boys she pointed out as 'nice' or 'cute'. I went out with her once, to a university bar, and sat nursing a single Lemon Bacardi

Breezer while the others drank and laughed. Sarah kept urging me to drink more, to loosen up, but I didn't want to lose control. I couldn't force myself to enjoy it. I skipped most of it, already feeling detached.

The isolation set in quickly. I stopped going out with Sarah, spending more and more time in my room. My training sessions in the gym became my main focus. The courses, accountancy, economics and business administration, were far from exciting, and I struggled to muster any interest in the lectures. My mind was constantly elsewhere, focused on racing. Even there, things felt uncertain. We didn't have the money for a clear testing programme in Formula Ford, and without a plan, I couldn't see a path forward. It was a stark contrast to the momentum I'd had coming off a strong final season in karting. Now, everything felt like it was stalling.

The weight of it all began to take its toll. I felt stuck, like I didn't belong at university, but without a way to fully throw myself into racing, I was adrift. The stress, the uncertainty and the growing isolation eventually took a physical toll too.

It started as a sore throat and just feeling a bit under the weather, something I'd experienced plenty of times before. I took some over-the-counter medicine and carried on as usual. But what began as mild symptoms developed into a persistent sore throat and body aches. I hate having a sore throat – the kind where you can't even swallow without discomfort. Even so, I kept pushing through, going to the gym and attending lectures. But it wouldn't go away. Slowly, it became clear that I couldn't keep up. I stopped training because my body just wasn't up to it.

By January, after the Christmas break, things worsened. The days in Edinburgh were cold and windy, and even the thought of bundling up to leave my room felt exhausting. I started skipping lectures, unable to muster the energy to get out of bed. Weeks went by, and my symptoms only intensified. My parents insisted I see a doctor. Reluctantly, I went to the university clinic, where the doctor initially thought it was just the flu. Blood tests revealed a low white blood cell count, and I was eventually diagnosed with glandular fever.

In some ways, it was a relief to know what was wrong. But it only compounded my deep feeling of unhappiness. I couldn't train, I couldn't study properly, and I spent most of my time lying in bed. I started to gain weight. I was never interested in cooking so lived off mushed-up muesli, though I at least opted for the sugar-free version. I was physically drained, emotionally stuck, and the feeling of doing nothing left me spiralling.

It took months to recover, and during that time, I started to question everything. My lectures, when I managed to go to them, felt meaningless – huge accounting spreadsheets and profit-and-loss statements that seemed to have no relevance to the life I wanted. Growing up, I'd watched Mum and Dad run their shops with an entrepreneurial spirit, and this rigid, corporate world I was being taught felt utterly foreign. My interest in my studies faded, and every lecture became a struggle. Still, I pushed through. I couldn't let myself fail. Even in that fog of unhappiness, I refused to acknowledge those feelings or let them derail me. I passed my exams with good marks, of course I did, but it was more out of discipline than any real engagement with the material.

I was just existing, going through the motions. It wasn't a life, and it certainly wasn't the life of a young student in her first year at university, or a young driver who had come fifteenth in the World Karting Championship. But I knew I would have to find a way through. The turning point came when I discovered an opportunity for a student accommodation exchange with Trinity College Dublin for the summer holidays. It was the perfect chance to be reunited with Wayne Douglas, who was based out there, and to take up an instructor role at Mondello Park, Ireland's famous racetrack. For the first time in months, I had something to look forward to – a spark of motivation that I desperately needed. My body had given me the clearest signal that I was unhappy and that forced me to stop, to reset, but now I could see a way forward. The unhappiness lingered, but for the first time in months, I saw a way out.

I loved Dublin as a city, it was somewhere new and fresh with no connection to my unhappiness at university. There was an openness about Dubliners, a willingness to include you, that put me at ease almost instantly. At Mondello Park I felt like I was back with my people – racing people, people I belonged with. I worked as an instructor, sometimes helping guests get behind the wheel and other times just moving cars around the track. The job paid £80 a day, and I would have worked every day if I could have, but bookings weren't consistent. I'd always look forward to the call asking if I could come;

the other instructors, most of whom were Irish, were great craic and the day would fly by.

Mondello Park wasn't just about work. It introduced me to a group of young Irish racers who brought a lightness and humour I hadn't experienced in the racing world before. James Murphy, known as Murfster, became a close friend, and the others had an ease about them – a non-judgemental, welcoming energy that was a stark contrast to the animosity I'd faced in karting. I felt comfortable, and when I started showing pace in testing, I earned their respect. Gone was the nagging doubt about whether I was quick or belonged there.

I poured my student loan into testing, scraping together enough for two days on the track. After one session Wayne, not one to sugarcoat anything, started shouting at me in the back of the truck about something I'd done wrong on track.

I snapped back, *You can criticise me all you want, but don't shout at me. Talk to me.* Mum and Dad had never shouted at me and I didn't respond to that type of aggression. From then on, our relationship solidified. He had a sharp sense of humour too. I remember once talking about my student accommodation.

He looked at me and said, *Do you have a mirror in your room?*

Yeah, of course.

You might want to start using it.

Coming from someone who looked like he had been dragged through a hedge backwards, it was a wake-up call. And hilarious.

As the summer drew to a close, the dread of returning to university began to creep in. The racetrack had reignited the spark in me, my love of racing, and the pull was undeniable. A new reality began to set in – this was where I belonged. The life I wanted wasn't in lecture halls or spreadsheets.

When I returned to Edinburgh, I moved into the flat Sarah had found for us. I hadn't contributed at all to the search, something I meekly apologised for. She showed me my room and my heart sank – it was painted black. I couldn't stand the idea of spending even a minute in that room.

I pushed through, feeling obliged to carry on – we had been brought up not to be quitters. Mum and Dad came down to help me repaint the room white, and I signed up for all my lectures, determined to start the new academic year as planned. But by the second week, sitting in a packed economics lecture hall with over 200 other students, it hit me: *What am I doing here?* I felt like a sheep following the flock, doing what everyone told me I should do. My goal was to be a racing driver, but here I was, stuck on a path that felt entirely wrong.

For the first time ever, I walked out of a lecture early. Me – the disciplined one who never quit anything – stood up and left. There were no tears, no sadness, just a quiet but intense realisation: I have to take control of my life. For the first time, that meant quitting. I walked and walked, through the streets of Edinburgh and into Holyrood Park, mulling over my next move. Finally, I sat on a bench and mustered up the courage to call home. Dad answered.

I've got something to tell you, I said.

I know, Toots, he replied. *You want to leave university.*

Yes, I said simply.

Okay, he said. *Pack your things. I'll come and get you tomorrow morning, but by then you need to have a plan of what you're going to do.*

A weight lifted from my shoulders. I hadn't really unpacked, so it didn't take long to get everything ready. That night, I didn't sleep while I worked out what I needed to do. The first step was to tell the head of my year that I was leaving university. I hadn't had much interaction with him before, so there was no awkwardness or hesitation as I walked into his office. When I told him, quite confidently, that I was leaving university to become a racing driver, he raised his eyebrows and said, *Really?*

Yes, I replied, explaining my need to focus entirely on my racing career.

He listened, and to my surprise, he smiled and said, *Well, you know what? That sounds great. But I'll keep your place open on the course. If anything changes in the next twelve months, you'll always have the option to come back.*

It was a kind gesture but, deep down, I knew there was no way I was coming back. My decision was final, and my focus was entirely on the path ahead. I walked out of his office, ready to take the leap.

By the time Dad arrived, I knew: I was going to move to Silverstone, the heart of British motorsport, where the F1 Grand Prix took place and, in its vicinity, the bases of most motorsport teams. I would find somewhere to stay, work as an instructor and focus entirely on my racing.

The following week, with all my worldly possessions jam packed into my parents' Golf TDI – their pride and joy – I made the eight-hour drive to Northampton. Mum and Dad had given me the car, sacrificing it for an older one that had belonged to Granny and Grandpa, so I could make this move. I blasted music the whole way. The drive felt like freedom – finally, I was following my own path.

Once in Northampton, I stopped at a newsagent's and scoured the local paper for accommodation. I found a listing for a room in a bungalow owned by an elderly woman. When I visited, she greeted me warmly, showed me the room, and listened patiently as I explained I'd be out most of the time because I was a racing driver. *Silverstone's not far from here*, she said with a smile, and just like that, I had a place to stay.

The first job I found was as a marshal at the Silverstone karting track, earning £5 an hour. I was positioned at the end of a short straight to wave flags of warning – yellow for spins, blue for get out of the way. It was long hours, and no matter the weather, I was at my post. I remember one particularly freezing evening when my hands were shaking so badly I bought a hot chocolate and a Dairy Milk bar at the café during my break to warm up, only to realise I'd spent almost my entire hour's wages. It was a humbling start.

A few weeks later, I got a call from James Murphy, whom I'd met at Mondello Park. He told me about a room that had just become available with two Northern Irish racers, Adam

Carroll and Tim Mullen. Within two days, I moved out of the bungalow and into a house of racing drivers. Adam was chasing a career in Formula Three and Tim was an established GT driver. The energy in that house was electric – focused, driven, and filled with the camaraderie of people who lived for racing. Not long after, I secured a job as an instructor at PalmerSport, one of the leading corporate race centres. For the first time, everything felt aligned. I was fully immersed in the world of motorsport, surrounded by people who shared my passion.

When I moved into the house, the hierarchy was clear. Tim, being the oldest and most established, had the biggest room. Adam, his cousin, took the second biggest, leaving me with the smallest room. It didn't matter. I had enough space, and I was just happy to be there. If they thought having a girl in the house might mean some domestic advantages, they were in for a shock. I wasn't at all domesticated and couldn't cook, a fact they quickly discovered to their disappointment.

We were part of a larger group of racing drivers living near Silverstone, and our evenings followed a routine. We'd decide whose house we were eating at, head to the supermarket together and buy dinner. If we had extra money, it was steaks or chicken. If funds were tight, it was pasta with homemade tomato sauce. Adam was the best cook. My only contribution was washing up.

Despite getting along well, it was still a typical house share. Tim, who loved Ginger Nuts and was a ginger himself, would count how many were left in his packet and get annoyed if anyone stole one. The milk was another battleground; finishing it and not replacing it was practically a crime.

Mum and Dad had given me a credit card for emergencies, but I saw it as a matter of pride not to use it. Every month, I calculated how many days I needed to work to make ends meet. Between my job at PalmerSport, shifts as a marshal at the karting track and a third job as a sales assistant at Grand Prix Racewear, a small shop near the track selling racing equipment and helmets, I managed to scrape by.

My days were busy, but I always carved out time to train, often getting up early before work to fit it in. On days off, I would join the rest of the group and we would often head to Northampton or Milton Keynes, usually to look around the shops, go to the cinema and, budget permitting, eat out.

Most of the time, I was in uniform for work or training gear when I went to the gym. On the rare occasions we went out – whether to celebrate someone's strong race result or a birthday – I was hit with the same feeling: I had nothing to wear and hadn't really figured out my style. My budget didn't help. After covering my living costs, there was little left for anything extra, let alone the clothes I saw in shop windows. It took me weeks to save up for a single pair of Diesel jeans.

But I never felt hard done by. Within the group, I'd become the little sister – the one everyone looked out for. Still, I was shaped by my karting days, when I overheard drivers talking about girls. It stayed with me. I knew those divisions still existed. I would hear the boys talk about girls in the same way. If I crossed the line into having any kind of relationship with one of them, I'd be put in that same category – and I had always wanted to be seen as a racing driver first. My racing meant so much to me, and that influenced all of my relationships. I absolutely wasn't going to date a racing driver.

At PalmerSport, we always had to be at the autodrome in Bedford by 8 a.m. It was in the middle of nowhere, so it took forty-five minutes to drive there on a good day and over an hour on a bad one. To make sure I was never late – I hated being late, especially since it meant getting the worst jobs of the day – I left the house at 7 a.m. on the dot. Sometimes, I'd even wake up at 5.30 a.m. to squeeze in training before the commute.

The worst days were when I was assigned to the Caterhams, especially in the rain. The open cars meant we had to suit up in rain gear, and it was always cold and wet. On the other hand, getting the Renault Clio Cup cars was a highlight – they were covered, nimble and much more enjoyable to drive. The guests were divided into six groups and revolved around six stations, each of which had a different track layout and car to drive. Each group had a team leader, who was always a woman, and they wore white trousers with red fleeces, while we instructors wore black trousers with red fleeces. As the only female instructor, I often saw the hesitation on the guests' faces, silently hoping they wouldn't get 'the girl'.

One day, a guest didn't bother keeping his thoughts to himself.

He brazenly told Esther, the team leader, *Please don't give me the girl.*

I gave Esther a nod, and she gave me a wry smile – I wanted him in my car. From the moment he stepped out of the bus, he was loud and cocky, laughing with his friends about how he'd be quicker than his instructor. When we got to the car, he ignored anything I said, brushing off my instructions and claiming he already knew what to do.

I've got this, he said dismissively.

Oh, I've got this too, I thought.

By then, I knew exactly how this was going to play out. Out on the track, it quickly became clear, as expected, that his confidence was misplaced. Despite his bravado, his lines were sloppy, and he overestimated his abilities at every corner. He worked through his practice laps. When his first timed lap came around, which would determine the leaderboard, my finger hovered over the kill switch – a button between us designed to cut the engine in emergencies. Just as we approached the fastest corner, I tapped the switch. The car lost drive, the rear tyres skidded and he lost the back end. Completely baffled, face white as a sheet, he asked what had happened.

Looks like you carried too much speed into the corner, I said dismissively.

To end the session, instructors always did a lap to demonstrate the perfect racing line. Normally, I drove at about 80 per cent, but he was going to get 99 per cent. Late braking, sliding the car through corners, using every inch of the track. He braced himself as we hurtled towards the end of the straight; his foot slammed the floor, hitting an imaginary brake pedal as if convinced I was braking too late. When we climbed out of the car, he could barely look at me. His awkwardness was broken only by Esther's voice: *So, did you have a good time?*

Most guests, however, had no issue. One day Phil, the head instructor, pulled me aside and asked me to sign an NDA.

We've got some special guests coming, he said, *and you'll be looking after one of them in the Renault Clio Cup cars – your speciality.*

We waited at the main building near the entrance, still unsure who our special guests would be. Two motorbikes appeared, flanked by blacked-out cars. The riders removed their helmets, revealing two of the most recognisable faces in the world: Prince William and Prince Harry. Jeans, shirts, no fuss – just two brothers casually arriving at a racetrack. Phil assigned me to William.

The competitive energy between the brothers was palpable from the start.

I said to William, *So, I guess we need to make sure you beat your brother.*

Ever gracious, he replied, with a polite smile, *Well, that would be nice.*

It was clear from the start that William and Harry had very different characters. William was thoughtful and considered, while Harry was the more extroverted of the two, gung-ho and full of energy. At one point, he jumped out of a car, climbed onto the bonnet and started waving his jumper around his head, clearly enjoying the moment. William found it hilarious, their rivalry tempered by an obvious camaraderie.

When it came to driving, Harry had raw speed – he was naturally fast – but he couldn't put together a clean lap when it mattered. William, by contrast, was more methodical, steadily improving and cutting down his time with each lap. By the end of the session, William had nailed a strong lap, just beating Harry's time. As we parted, William, smiling, thanked me. Job done.

With my own racing, the Formula Ford testing had been a solid start, but putting together the budget for a full season of racing was proving more challenging than ever. The focus shifted to building a budget, with the plan to move straight into Formula Renault, the next category up. We needed to find £125,000. A lot of money.

In the junior categories, winter is all about the scramble – teams looking for the best drivers, and drivers doing everything they can to secure a seat with the best teams. The months are filled with endless phone calls, rumours flying and constant negotiations. Everyone's trying to figure out who their teammates will be, how much pre-season testing they can afford, and what it'll take to get race-ready.

By the start of 2002, it was clear we didn't have the budget to get into a top team. In fact, it wasn't even certain we'd have enough to finish the season. But I was desperate to get back out there. Paul had secured some funding, and Mum and Dad said they would step in to cover the second and third payments, giving me the reassurance that, at the very least, I had a season of racing ahead.

The problem with limited pre-season testing, though, is that you don't start the season well prepared. And in motorsport, the harsh truth is simple: the more money you have, the faster you go. It became glaringly obvious that we had a massive uphill battle ahead of us – not enough track time, not a top team and a long way from the front of the grid.

6

My first year in Formula Renault was a learning year. I wasn't in a top team, didn't have a teammate to share data with and lacked the experience to make up for it. But I was back on the grid, and that gave me hope. Hope that I could show what I was capable of and build some momentum. I scraped into the top ten a couple of times – enough to get noticed. Being in the paddock meant I could start talking with the top teams and lay the groundwork for the following season.

But, towards the end of the summer, the money had run out. We couldn't afford to finish the last few races, so we turned our focus to the following year. The goal was the Motorworld team. Their black-and-yellow cars were iconic, and they had the reputation as being front-runners. Paul teamed up with a marketing agency called Purple Tangerine to help secure sponsorship, and they landed on BT, which was launching broadband – proof of just how long ago this was. The discussions looked promising, and for the first time in a while, things felt like they were starting to click.

In 2003, when I was twenty years old, I joined Motorworld. This time, I had strong teammates and access to data, which was a game-changer. For someone like me, who thrived on structure and preparation, it was everything. I threw myself into it, studying data, making detailed notes on every track, and working out exactly where I needed to improve.

The season opener was at Snetterton in Norfolk, a track I knew well. I started with two top-ten finishes, giving me a solid start and some confidence. But a race mid-season, back at Snetterton, marked my breakthrough. I'd been quick in testing, fast enough to be tipped for pole. Qualifying was tight, and I ended up fifth, with Lewis Hamilton, already dominating the championship, on pole.

At the start, I got a strong launch off the grid, moving into fourth almost immediately. By the first lap, as we approached the Bomb Hole – a fast, sweeping right-hander – I saw an opening on the inside. Without a second thought, I went for it, diving through and taking third. From there, I was chasing Lewis Hamilton and James Rossiter, two of the strongest drivers that season. I crossed the line in third place.

Standing on the podium, trophy in hand, I saw Mum and Dad in the crowd, looking emotional. It felt like I'd finally shown the promise they had always believed in, like I'd repaid their faith. Then came the champagne. Lewis, already well versed in celebrations with eight podium finishes and five wins that season, had to help me open my bottle before I could join in. It was a small thing, but it summed up where I was – just starting to find my place.

The season ended strongly for me, culminating in being named as one of the six finalists for the British Young Driver of the Year Award – the first time a female driver had ever been nominated. The award would be decided by a shootout, with the six drivers setting times in a Formula Three car, a German Touring Car (known as DTM – Deutsche Tourenwagen Masters) and a British Touring Car, at Silverstone. The media started to take notice. There was a buzz around me, and for the first time, I had real momentum.

The British Racing Drivers' Club (BRDC), which ran the award and owns Silverstone, was an old-school, male-dominated institution – a gentleman's club in every sense. Its prestigious clubhouse, right at the heart of Silverstone, was a place I'd never set foot in before. Walking through the reception on the first day of the shootout, I was struck by the walls lined with portraits of legendary racing drivers, none of them women. It hit me then: being the first female to be nominated for this award wasn't just a step – it was a monumental moment.

I wasn't going to be sharing the changing room with the other finalists as we suited up. Instead, I was shown to a separate room. On the table was a large bouquet of flowers. Opening the note, I saw it was from the chairwoman of the British Women Racing Drivers Club – an organisation born from the fact that women had only been allowed to join the BRDC eight years earlier. The note read, *We're all so proud of you. Go out there and show them what you can do.*

It gave me a sense that I wasn't alone. Standing in that room, in the heart of a place so steeped in tradition, I realised just how much it meant to be there, fighting for such a prestigious award. It wasn't just about me – it felt bigger than that.

Our mobile phones were taken from us as soon as we arrived, setting the tone for what lay ahead. For two days, every move we made was being analysed, how we carried ourselves, how we prepared before getting in the car, and every moment in the car itself was under scrutiny. The judges had access to all our data, and nothing escaped their attention.

We were also put through a series of interviews with the judges, each one intense and deliberate. There was a lot of secrecy surrounding the process; lap times weren't shared, so none of us could compare ourselves to the others.

It became clear that the judges were looking at the bigger picture – who had the best attitude, who showed the most improvement, who adapted to the conditions and who gave the most incisive feedback to the engineers. Everything was being reported back to the judges, so even the smallest of interactions in the garage carried weight.

The winner would be announced at the Autosport Awards at Grosvenor House on London's Park Lane in the middle of December, a long wait after such a tense few days. This is still one of the most glamorous events in motorsport, a black-tie evening where the audience is a who's who of Formula One, rallying and every major category of racing. The Autosport Young Driver of the Year Award is the pinnacle at the end of the evening – a launchpad for future stars, with past winners such as David Coulthard and Jenson Button.

I drove down to London on the day of the awards. Having missed out on the years of going out or having any events to really dress up for, I was completely out of my comfort zone that evening. I'd bought a black dress from a shop in Northampton. My budget didn't stretch to anything particularly extravagant. The sequined halterneck dress was simple but safe, and I hoped it wouldn't stand out too much among the tuxedos the other finalists would be wearing. But when it came to my hair, I had no clue. I just pulled it back like I always did, figuring it was the easiest solution.

Makeup was another challenge entirely. I barely wore any on a daily basis, so the idea of creating a 'special evening look' wasn't even on my radar. I kept it basic, adding some mascara and a bit of lip gloss, hoping it would be enough to show I had made an effort. As I got ready in the hotel, I couldn't shake the feeling that I was winging it. Everything about the evening felt like uncharted territory – I wasn't polished, I wasn't glamorous enough, but I was there, and that was what mattered.

Arriving at Grosvenor House the scale of the evening hit me. As I walked through the grand entrance, I saw my face flashing up alongside the other five finalists on giant screens. My picture was plastered alongside images of iconic racing drivers who were also up for awards that night.

We had taken a table for the evening with eight spots, a chance to bring together all the people who had helped me on the journey so far. Mum, Dad and my brother, of course, but also Paul, who, alongside Nigel from Purple Tangerine, had been instrumental in finding the budget to get me racing that season. Duncan White, who had guided me through the karting years, was there too. I was the second driver he'd worked with to make it to the Young Driver of the Year Award, and it was a proud moment for both of us. It wasn't just a night for me, sitting at that table surrounded by people who had believed in me – it felt special for all of us.

At the start of the evening, we were called up on stage to be introduced to the audience by the host, BBC sports presenter Steve Rider. The other five finalists lined up beside me as their names were read out one by one. Then Steve paused, looked at the lineup, and said, *But we're missing a finalist. Where's our sixth finalist?*

I stepped slightly forward, trying not to look self-conscious, and said, *Well, I'm the sixth finalist. My name is Susie Stoddart.* Steve looked at me, clearly caught off guard, and with a laugh said, *That's right. We have a girl in the competition this year.*

There was a ripple of laughter from the audience, and I had no choice but to laugh along. I was used to moments like this by now. But as I stood there, I realised: *You haven't won, Susie.* If he didn't even know there was a girl in the competition, he most certainly knew that a girl wasn't taking home the award.

As we walked off stage and into the green room, I found myself surrounded by legends of the sport, all getting ready to make their appearances. Among them was Sir Jackie Stewart and his wife, Lady Helen, who glided over to me, the picture of elegance in a room where women were few and far between. She gave me a kind smile, leaned in slightly and asked in that poised, polite way, *My dear, why would you want to be a racing driver?*

I fumbled out some standard answer about my love of racing, but her question lingered. It wasn't said unkindly, but it held that air of genuine curiosity mixed with disbelief.

The prize for the award itself was significant – £50,000 towards the next season's budget and a Formula One test with McLaren. It was career-changing, and as much as I was proud to be there, I had always known deep down that it wasn't my award to win – I still had more to prove. I hadn't yet shown everyone what I was capable of. At that point, there was still a gap between where I was and being a true front-runner – one who could fight for podiums every race weekend. I knew I could get there, though. Offers from top teams for the following season were already coming in. With the continued financial backing of BT, it was decided that I would stay in Formula Renault for another year and aim to fight for the championship.

One week later, *Autosport* magazine came out, and I remember flipping through the pages to its coverage of the awards night. The event looked so glamorous – drivers in sharp tuxedos, the drivers' wives in stunning dresses. And there I was, in my budget black dress, hair tied back, barely any makeup. I didn't fit the image, and not in a way I could shrug off. It hit me that if I wanted to stand out, it needed to be for the right reasons.

Shortly after, Nigel from Purple Tangerine called me in for a meeting. He was polite but direct, walking me through the reality of what it would take to attract sponsors.

You're going to be in the spotlight more now, he said. *We need to think about how you present yourself. Sponsors are watching, and image matters.* He talked about upcoming photoshoots and the narrative they wanted to build around me as a driver.

*   *   *

It was clear what they were after – this 'sexy female driver' angle that made me squirm. It wasn't me, and it wasn't what I wanted to be known for. But I also understood the harsh reality: without sponsorship, there was no racing. If this was what it took to keep my career alive, I had to find a compromise. Femininity wasn't something I'd ever played up, but now it seemed like I had to embrace it.

That meeting and the pictures from the awards were a wake-up call. I realised I couldn't keep ignoring my image. Things needed to change. I'd been living like one of the guys, eating the same portions of pasta, indulging without much thought, and it was starting to show. I had been training hard and getting fitter, but I'd also got bigger. I was going to clean up my diet, focus on my training, and make this my year. I didn't want to just survive under the spotlight; I wanted to thrive in it. This wasn't about becoming someone I wasn't, but about stepping into a version of myself that could handle everything the sport demanded – on and off the track. And it paid off.

The 2004 Formula Renault season was a year where everything came together. I'd joined Comtec Racing, one of the top teams, run by the legendary Jonathan Lewis. The cars were instantly recognisable, blue with a striking yellow splash on the nose, and were synonymous with success in junior formulas. My teammate, Wesley Barber, was considered one of the championship favourites, and the team had built a reputation as a force to be reckoned with. From the outset, there was an energy about us, a sense that we were the ones to watch.

Jonathan and his wife, who managed the team's operations, created a family-like atmosphere that was as supportive as it was competitive. When I visited their workshop in Norfolk to review data or prepare with my engineer, I stayed at their house. It was clear they believed in me. Even when the budget felt tight, the team ensured I had the testing and resources needed to compete at the front.

The season kicked off at Thruxton, one of the fastest and most demanding circuits on the calendar, and by the time we reached Brands Hatch, everything clicked. In the first final, I finished second, locked in a nose-to-tail battle with my team-mate Wesley. In the second final, I stood on the podium again, taking third. Two podiums in one weekend – it was a statement, and suddenly, everyone was taking notice.

As the season progressed, the highs and lows of racing came into play. The momentum kept building. By the time we reached the final weekend at Donington, I had scored points in all races and was in contention for fourth in the championship, narrowly missing out by two points.

Through the season, I had to do a number of photoshoots, and every time, I had to grapple with this new sense of 'me': the female race driver the media wanted me to be, as well as who I wanted to be for myself, on my own terms. There was one shoot that crystallised this for me: a shoot for the *Sunday Times* 'One to Watch' feature. I was greeted by the makeup artist, stylist and photography team, and they led me to the clothing rack, unveiling the wardrobe they'd picked out for me.

I started flicking through the options: leather jumpsuits, tiny shorts, crop tops. With every piece, my stomach sank a little further. I kept thinking, *I can't wear this. No way.* I was willing to step out of my comfort zone, but this? This was too far. As we went through the rack, it became clear there wasn't a single thing I could imagine myself putting on.

Eventually, they asked me what I wanted to try first, and I had to be honest, telling them, *There's nothing here I'm going to wear.* What followed was a slightly awkward huddle between the creative team and me, trying to figure out a compromise. In the end, we agreed the best option was for me to wear my racing suit. I loved the pictures.

Other photoshoots followed a similar pattern, but sponsorship kept me racing, and if this was what they needed in order to sell me, I was willing to play along – up to a point. But I always knew my limits, and I never let anyone push me past them.

Looking back, I realise those limits have shifted over time. I've grown into myself, learned that I don't have to conform to anyone else's projections. But back then, I was caught in the reality of motorsport – a world where image is as much a part of the game as lap times. Motorsport had always been about image, and at that time, the only women visible in the sport were the pit girls, standing trackside in tiny outfits, holding umbrellas. I had to find another way through.

There was no doubt I'd be nominated again for the Young Driver of the Year Award after such a strong season, but this time, I was ready. I knew what I was walking into, what was expected of me, and I was there to win.

I arrived at Silverstone for the shootout and was told I would be starting in the German Touring Car. Walking into the garage, I saw the same chief engineer as the year before, a big burly German. I went over to shake his hand, but he glanced at me, then said, *Oh, there's a girl in the competition again this year.*

I smiled politely and said, *Yes, it's me again.*

He frowned, shaking his head in disbelief.

No, no, it's not you. Last year's girl was . . . he said, puffing out his cheeks and stretching his arms wide to demonstrate someone larger.

I stared at him for a moment, letting his words settle, then replied, *Yes, that was me. I've just lost a bit of weight since then.*

He stumbled over his words, clearly embarrassed. I wasn't offended – I'd spent years dealing with boyish banter like this and wasn't about to let it faze me. I didn't own a set of scales, but I knew I'd lost at least 10 kilos since the previous year. All the hard work, training and eating better had paid off, and it showed – not just in how I looked but in how I felt.

By the time the awards night rolled around again, everything felt different. On the table were the same people as before, but I had been loaned an expensive gold-and-silver dress, one that made me feel as glamorous as anyone in the room. I'd brought in a professional to do my hair and makeup. I also stayed at the Grosvenor Hotel to make things as seamless as possible. When I walked into that grand ballroom, it felt like a completely different experience from the year before. When I was called up on stage, there was no hesitation, no fumbling over who the girl was. Steve Rider looked me in the eye, called my name without pause, and I stepped forward with confidence.

Standing there, I felt no doubt about my place in that group. My season had been strong, my performances had spoken for themselves, and I knew I'd earned the right to stand alongside the best. I was nervous because I really wanted to win, desperately hoping to hear my name called out. As the ceremony built to its climax, the whole table was tense. When it came time to announce the winner, we all joined hands, silently willing it to be me.

My name wasn't called.

The disappointment stung. As I got up to leave the table, one of the judges pulled me to the side and said, *It was close – really close. You nearly had it.*

I didn't want to hang around for the party, preferring to go back to my room. I had nothing to celebrate, but I didn't need the award to confirm what I already knew: I was ready. Ready for Formula Three – the category that had ignited my dreams when I watched in awe less than ten years ago as a thirteen-year-old girl at Donington.

At that point, Formula One no longer felt like an impossible dream. It was two steps away. For the first time, it felt within my grasp.

7

LIFE at home in Northampton was changing. Our group of friends, once buzzing with energy and shared dreams, was beginning to disband. For some, the racing journey was coming to an end, with the harsh world of motorsport becoming a reality. In our house, however, the dream was still alive. Adam Carroll had secured a test driver role with the Formula One team British American Racing, a monumental achievement that filled us all with pride. He was the first among us to breach the ranks of F1. I remember the evening he came home with his new team kit. We all huddled around, marvelling at his F1 race suit, embroidered with the names of various sponsors. Seeing one of our own make it to F1 brought it home – there was a tangible path, a real connection. If Adam could do it, I could too. We had all started in the same place, taken the same steps.

On my side, we explored several Formula Three teams before settling on Alan Docking Racing, a well-regarded outfit based at Silverstone. Alan was an Australian with a sterling reputation in junior motorsport; his team had clinched a Formula Three championship in 2002. An added bonus was their location at Silverstone – just twenty-five minutes from me. Any excuse to visit their workshop was enough. I'd often spend a few hours there at a time, getting to know the team and soaking up as much of the technical conversations between the engineer and mechanics as I could.

But Formula Three came with a daunting price tag: £500,000. BT continued to back me, offering a glimmer of hope, though we still hadn't secured the full budget to see the season through. Even so, on the strength of my 2004 season, optimism remained high that we'd find the support as the year progressed.

I had just turned twenty-one when I headed home to Oban for Christmas. It was a chance to spend time with my grandparents, which I treasured. Grandpa had recently passed away. It was the first death in our family and it hit me hard. I had been so lucky to grow up and spend a lot of time with all of my grandparents so at Christmas not seeing him in his usual chair left us all with a heavy sadness.

When I visited Gramps he always wanted to know every detail about my racing. Then I would sit down with Mo, with her delicious homemade oat crunch biscuits and a cup of tea. With her, I could open up, something I rarely did with anyone else. Our conversations were never about racing but about what was going on in my life.

In the New Year, I went to see Grandma, not liking the thought of her being alone. She mentioned she needed to go into town for milk and bread. The roads were icy, and I didn't want her risking the drive in those conditions.

I grabbed the keys and drove us to Bayview, a small corner shop, where we managed to park right out front – a stroke of luck on such a cold, icy day. She waited in the car while I headed inside.

Milk and bread in hand, I stepped outside, spotting her watching me with a smile. My feet slipped on some ice, and I hit the ground hard. The shock of the fall took my breath away, but as soon as I was over the shock, the pain in my left ankle – a sharp, searing agony – told me something was seriously wrong. I caught a glimpse of Grandma's alarmed face as she raced to me lying on the pavement. Her voice broke, *My dear, my dear, it's okay.*

It's not okay, Grandma . . . my ankle . . .

A small crowd had gathered by then. Two men helped lift me up, but the moment I stood, the pain shot through me. When I finally looked down, my foot dangled unnaturally, twisted at a grotesque angle that made my stomach churn. I couldn't process what I was seeing. Tears welled up as the reality started to sink in.

The ambulance arrived, but the ride to the hospital was a blur. At the hospital, there was a flurry of activity around me; a doctor took one look at my ankle and said bluntly, *We'll need to operate.*

I need my ankle to be okay.

Plates and pins will have to be inserted.

How long until I can race again?

A minimum of six weeks. And that's just to get back on your feet.

My mind raced to calculate the dates – I would miss pre-season testing. Was my year over before it had even begun? *No, no, no.* I pushed the thought out of my mind as if positive thinking would make me heal quicker. There's always a solution. *You just have to think about it properly*, I told myself. My dream that had felt so close now seemed to be slipping away. When Mum and Dad arrived, Mum took my hand immediately, worry etched on her face.

It's going to be okay, Suz.

The words barely registered as I closed my eyes. The operation was too complex to be done in Oban so an ambulance transported me to Glasgow.

The operation was as serious as the doctor had warned. Two metal plates and twelve pins were inserted to stabilise my shattered ankle and broken fibula. When I woke up from the anaesthesia, nausea hit me. I grabbed the cardboard kidney-shaped bowl and retched, spewing stomach bile – the only thing I had left. I tried to latch onto something. A solution, a hope, a way out, but instead, waves of sickness. Mum and Dad were by my side, trying to keep my spirits up, and at every opportunity, I pressed the surgeon.

How long will this take to heal?

A minimum of eight weeks, best case. The time period had increased with the seriousness of the injury, but there was also a warning: *If you rush this, you could do permanent damage.*

Eight weeks meant I would miss every crucial moment leading up to the season. Testing, preparation, building confidence in the car – all of it would be gone. If this wasn't devastating enough, the realisation that it was my left ankle – the one responsible for braking – added another layer of despair. Braking required immense force, and years of racing had built the strength in that leg to achieve the force needed to stamp late on the brake. Now, it felt as though all of that work had been undone in a single moment.

I refused to give up. I couldn't let it end like this. I clung to any shred of hope. If I could heal faster, if I could push through the pain, maybe, just maybe, I could salvage something.

Back in Oban, the isolation only deepened my sense of hopelessness. I felt stuck, miles away from the world I was chasing – nothing to grab onto. No hope. I became fixated on my recovery, clinging to the doctors' advice that nutrition could speed up the healing process. I asked Mum and Dad to prepare meals that were as clean and nutrient-packed as possible.

No carbs. Everything I eat has to help me recover faster.

They made me little tuna balls with lettuce and sweetcorn, but I'd only eat half. Mum would tell me I needed to eat more, but my appetite was gone, replaced by a single-minded focus: I needed to get back on my feet. The pain, however, was constant. My ankle throbbed relentlessly. Every step with crutches sent a dull ache radiating through my leg, the cold weather making it even worse. I could almost feel the metal plates shifting slightly with every move.

Rehabilitation began slowly. The doctors made it clear that my ankle needed at least three weeks to settle before I could even think about starting any serious physio. In the meantime,

I worked on my upper body to stay as fit as I could. But walking on crutches became my new reality.

We began seeking out specialists, chasing any solution that might speed up my recovery. Someone mentioned a hyperbaric oxygen chamber, so Mum and I made the long drive to a clinic in Norfolk that had one. I didn't fully understand the science, something about pressurised oxygen stimulating healing, but I was willing to try anything.

Lying inside the chamber was oddly calming. For an hour or so, I could do nothing but breathe deeply and imagine the oxygen working its magic on my battered ankle. It gave me a sliver of hope, even though I knew deep down that the first race of the season was slipping out of reach.

By late February, the odds of being ready were slim to none. That was when it started to dawn on me – a sinking feeling that I wasn't going to start this year's season after all, despite my very best efforts. I tried to make peace with the idea of joining a few races in, but even that hope began to fade as the timelines stretched further and further. The dream of that year became like a light at the end of the tunnel, growing dimmer and more distant as reality set in.

My left leg felt alien; as I tried to put more weight on my ankle, it became clear it had grown weak, the muscles deflated, useless and utterly incapable of supporting my weight. The whole leg had no power. But I kept going back to the chamber every second day, desperate for even the smallest improvement. Mum drove me there and back, always by my side.

After two weeks, it was clear the oxygen therapy wasn't the miracle I had hoped for. With Mum having to return to work, I chose to stay in Northampton rather than go back to Oban. The thought of being so distant from racing felt like I was giving up. Even though I couldn't drive or train properly, staying close to that world was my way of keeping the flame alive, however faint it had become.

I found a dedicated physio in Northampton and threw myself into the gruelling process of rebuilding strength. Progress was excruciatingly slow, far slower than I had hoped. To make matters worse, after my accident, I lost my racing licence. I couldn't compete without passing a medical test, and I knew I wasn't even close to being ready.

Not long after, a call came from Paul and Nigel. They were kind, but their message was blunt: without starting the season, securing sponsorship would be nearly impossible. And without sponsorship, there would be no racing.

The house in Northampton, once filled with friends and laughter, felt empty and lifeless. Adam was away most of the time with his F1 commitments, and Tim was now engaged and had moved out. The long, lonely nights were the hardest. As they dragged on, they became unbearable, with dark thoughts spiralling out of control. I'd drag myself up the twisting staircase on my backside, the crutches useless against its narrow turns. Each climb made me think of Gramps, confined to a wheelchair for years. His quiet stoicism, once something I admired, I now thought of as nothing short of heroic.

I struggled to fall asleep. The pain in my ankle would throb in sync with my heartbeat, and I'd count the hours until I could take another dose of painkillers. One night, the pain jolted me awake as I shifted in bed. Reaching for the pills, I realised I didn't have any water. Dragging myself to the bathroom, a wave of hopelessness crashed over me. Overwhelmed by the sheer unfairness of it all, I grabbed a crutch and slammed it against the floor, again and again, pouring every ounce of rage and frustration into each strike. I was sobbing uncontrollably, my breaths ragged, my body shaking, but I couldn't stop. I kept hammering it down until I had nothing left, until the anger gave way to something even heavier. My sobs took over, and I broke down completely, unable to hold back the flood of emotion any longer.

The first round of pre-season testing came and went. Word reached me that another driver had taken my seat. Then the first race at Donington passed by, just as quietly. My seat, my opportunity, the season I had poured everything into – gone. Slipped through my fingers.

I was a young woman who had spent nearly half her life chasing the dream of being a racing driver. If that dream was gone, then . . . who was I? In the midst of that void, I began a diary.

I was grasping at anything to make sense of what I was feeling. I bought a pack of Destiny cards. Glossy, brightly coloured astrological projections, promising cosmic guidance. I wasn't even sure I believed in them, but I desperately needed to believe in something. I needed a sign, however small, that maybe, just maybe, all wasn't lost.

I slept with Grandpa's cravat tucked under my pillow. It felt like holding onto him, to his memory, to his wisdom. In my diary, I signed off with a plea:

Please help me, Grandpa.

Looking back, I see those pages for what they were – a snapshot of one of my lowest points. My thoughts then weren't linear or logical; they were raw, untidy and filled with a kind of searching. I had done everything I could think of to keep going, to persevere, but it wasn't enough. I needed something external, something bigger than me, to give me hope, to fill the space where my own strength had been stretched too thin.

Eight weeks in and I was back in the doctor's office. The first time they removed the cast after one of the sessions, the specialist decided to assess my ankle's progress. The sight of it hit me like a gut punch. It was black and blue, grotesquely swollen and barely recognisable. I stared at it in disbelief. The doctor, however, seemed unfazed. He explained that getting the ankle moving was the only way to get back on my feet again.

Without hesitation, he grabbed my toes and began twisting and manipulating them, forcing movement back into the joint. The pain was excruciating, shooting through my leg. According to him, the agony was a necessary part of the recovery process. Pushing through it, he assured me, was the only way forward.

I gritted my teeth, biting down hard on the pain.

Go for it.

I told myself my pain threshold was equal to how much I wanted it, how much I wanted to get back in that car, racing. So I urged him to push harder.

But my determination had consequences. A week later, my go-hard or go-home approach came back to haunt me. A sharp, tearing pain shot through my leg – it turned out I'd ripped the fascia, the delicate layer of tissue that holds muscles in place. My refusal to let up had turned into a full-blown setback.

The aftermath left me with a permanent bulge on my left ankle – a not-so-subtle reminder that healing requires patience, not heroics. Sometimes, the bravest thing you can do is listen to your body and give it the time it needs.

I couldn't stand sitting in the house. That restless, trapped feeling started to get to me, so I decided to take on more hours at Grand Prix Racewear. It wasn't just about the job; I had to do anything to avoid being on my own. I'd already been working there part-time, but after my injury made instructing impossible it was my only option. Bruce, the manager, kindly picked me up in his car on his way to work.

Finally, he joked, *you can add that feminine touch to our dreadful window displays.* I hobbled around the shop on crutches, organising stock and arranging it into a neat display. All those hours spent in my mum's shop had prepared me well.

One morning, I arrived to find a large package from Sparco, the renowned Italian racing equipment manufacturer, which had sent over some items for our window display. As I unpacked, I pulled out a Kimi Räikkönen McLaren-Mercedes race suit and thought, *Perfect – this will grab attention.* The other suit was silver with a Mercedes star, featuring a German flag and the name Bernd Schneider embroidered on it. I glanced at it, thought, *No idea who that is*, and tossed it back into the box.

Somewhere deep inside, a flicker of determination started to burn brighter. In my diary, I began writing more words of encouragement to myself.

Stay strong. You can do this, Susie. Keep pushing.

Giving up wasn't an option – it never had been. There was something instinctive in me, an inner resolve woven into the fabric of who I was. No matter how hopeless things seemed, I just kept going. I refused to believe that everything I had worked for could be undone by one moment on an icy pavement. But even with that fire burning stronger again, the path forward remained unclear.

The one thing I could do was focus on getting my race licence back. I needed a victory, however big or small, and I decided this was going to be it: I was going to pass my medical. To pass, I needed to stand on my left leg for at least ten seconds. In training, five seconds became ten. I pushed past the pain until, at last, I reached twenty seconds. For the first time in months, I felt hopeful. If I could just get back into a racing car, maybe – just maybe – I could start to rebuild everything I had lost.

In the doctor's waiting room in Northampton, I started to focus my mind on anticipating the pain, absorbing the discomfort and putting on my game face. The doctor conducting the medical exam gave me a sympathetic look, clearly sensing my discomfort as I eased all my weight onto my left leg. My ankle throbbed, but I looked at him, not letting a grimace of pain appear on my face.

I stood on my left leg for ten seconds.

I stated it firmly, leaving no room for debate. He nodded, then proceeded to guide me through a series of range-of-motion tests, carefully assessing the mobility of my ankle. Finally, a lifeline. I had my racing licence back.

Soon, the question of how to get back into a racing car consumed every thought, narrowing the world to a single mission. There was no shortcut, but equally there was no waiting for an opportunity to present itself – it had to be pursued. Calls were made to every contact, every team that might listen. Among them was Jonathan Lewis, my former team boss. He spoke of a new championship, the World Series by Renault, and mentioned that the team owner, Pierre, had acquired a pair of Dallara chassis with Renault engines. Jonathan suggested helping with the initial shakedown of the cars – a foot in the door.

The shakedown led to an invitation for a full test. No financial contribution was requested, a rarity in motorsport. It was a gesture rooted in Jonathan's faith – his belief in my potential. After nine long months, the chance to drive again was finally here.

The first test at Donington was a stark awakening. The car demanded more – more power, more speed and far more physical strength than anything I had experienced before. By the end of the day, every muscle ached. It was clear the effort required was beyond me. My training had to intensify; the body had to catch up to the machine.

The second test at the Paul Ricard track, in the South of France, brought a new challenge. The track, with its sweeping lines and punishing speeds, had one corner, in particular, that was my nemesis. A fast right-hander with an unforgiving bump midway through – I simply couldn't hold on. With no power steering and every vibration from the track reverberating through my body, I was at my limit. Retreating to the solitude of the women's toilets, I broke down. With tears streaming down my face, I leaned my head against the cold wall of the toilet cubicle. My fists rested there for a moment before I started hammering them against it, the frustration spilling out. I wasn't driving the car; it was driving me. I needed to dig deep and find a way to take back control.

The next time I approached the bump, I locked my left elbow against the side of the cockpit, bracing myself to absorb the force. It was the only way for me to get through the corner. As Grandma would say: *It wasn't pretty, but it got the job done.*

There's a truth about motorsport that nothing, not even the most rigorous training, can fully replicate the physical toll of driving a race car. Test day by test day, I started to feel stronger. Each session was a step towards reclaiming the confidence I had lost. By the end of the year, I had completed nearly twenty test days. Jonathan and his wife had taken me under their wing. Pierre, the team's owner, was committed to having me in the car for the upcoming season. The clouds that had hung over me for so long began to lift. I felt like I was finally back where I belonged: behind the wheel, fighting for my dream.

As 2006 approached, I was hungry to get racing again. The World Series by Renault signified a significant leap – not just for me but for the entire team. Preparations were in overdrive: the car was primed, and I was back in peak form. Every piece of the puzzle was slotting into place, and the momentum was building.

Then came the call. Jonathan asked me to meet them at the workshop in Norfolk. I assumed it was a final planning session before the first test, but as I sat down with Jonathan, his wife and Pierre, the mood in the room was heavy. They had spent the holidays crunching the numbers, and the news hit like a hammer blow. The budget for the season was a daunting £500,000. They had gone above and beyond, contributing as much as they could, but there was still a £200,000 shortfall – and I had to find it. Without that funding, the season simply wouldn't happen.

Outside the workshop, I sat in my car in silence, staring at the dashboard as the enormity of the situation sank in. The first test was just ten days away, and the first race only six weeks off. Where was I supposed to find that kind of money? I picked up the phone and called home.

Dad answered, his voice calm but clouded with concern as I poured everything out.

What am I going to do, Dad?

There was a long pause.

I don't know, Toots.

Hearing those words from the man who always had a solution felt like the final blow. For the first time, it truly felt like the road might end here. While I was on the phone with Dad, another call came through. I glanced at the number – +49 – international, but I couldn't immediately place the country. I quickly told Dad I had to go and answered the call.

Is this Susie Stoddart?

Yes, I said, intrigued by the German accent at the other end of the line.

This is Gerhard Ungar from Mercedes-Benz Motorsport. What do you think of DTM?

I thought back to the test I'd done during the Young Driver of the Year Award.

Well, I think it's great.

What are you doing tomorrow?

I paused, caught off guard.

Actually, it's just freed up.

Good. Get yourself to Barcelona. We want to test you.

8

WITH my carry-on case in one hand and helmet bag in
the other, I walked through the arrivals hall at
Barcelona airport. That's when I spotted him – a man in the
unmistakable silver Mercedes-Benz uniform, the star
stitched on the right side of his chest. He gave me a firm
handshake.

You're Susie Stoddart? he asked in a thick German accent.

Yes, I replied, following him to the car.

So, you're in marketing, hospitality or catering? he continued,
raising an eyebrow.

I froze for a moment; he couldn't have got the memo.

No, I said. *I'm here to drive the DTM car.*

His expression shifted slightly, eyebrows furrowing in what
I could only interpret as surprise.

Oh, was all he replied as we set off. Well versed in being
mistaken as anybody but a racing driver, I shrugged it off.

Driving into the paddock in Barcelona, the first thing that
struck me was the sheer scale of it all. Ahead were ten massive
silver Mercedes trucks. Seeing them, the significance of

where I was hit me. German touring cars, particularly in the 2000s, were a huge part of the motorsport world. DTM wasn't just another championship, it was the leading touring car championship in Europe, with high-profile manufacturers like Audi, BMW and Mercedes-Benz fighting for dominance. These cars, though based on production models, were engineering masterpieces – with sophisticated aerodynamics and powerful engines. It was fast, technical and fiercely competitive.

Mercedes-Benz, one of the biggest manufacturers in the world, a brand synonymous with engineering excellence, and here I was – testing for them. But I wasn't intimidated. I had nothing to lose in that moment. I was just so grateful to be there. I wasn't worried about what could go wrong because there was nothing to lose. This was just a test – an opportunity to grab hold of. Twenty-four hours earlier, I had nothing, and now I was about to test a Mercedes-Benz factory car. There are different types of nerves – the kind that make your stomach knot with fear, and the kind that fuel you. Flight or fight. And I was ready to fight.

I was led straight to Gerhard Ungar. There was no small talk – this was the German way, I would discover. He shook my hand.

Do you have your kit?

Yes.

You need a seat. Get one fitted.

Okay, but just one thing. Will there be time for me to walk the track?

You don't know the track? He looked astonished.

No.

I'd never stepped foot here, not even to watch a race. I had studied a track map on the plane and watched some videos, but that was all I had. He disappeared into the garage and reappeared with none other than Mika Häkkinen – a two-time Formula One World Champion.

Mika, take this girl around the track.

The only time I had seen Mika was while I was watching Formula One on television and now I was sitting next to him in the passenger seat hurtling round a track.

So, at the end you turn right.

Thanks, Mika, very helpful.

He gave me a wry smile. I laughed and the ice was broken.

If the Germans were direct, then the Finns are like their furniture – minimal and functional.

Brake here. Watch this kerb. More here. Less there.

Back in the paddock, it was time to suit up. I spotted someone nearby and asked where I could change. He gestured towards the back of a truck, and the mechanics and engineers inside stepped out, giving me a moment of privacy.

I walked into the garage, helmet in hand, standing still for a moment as the activity buzzed around me. A sea of men, all chatting in German, working, while I stood there as the lone woman. It wasn't something I often thought about, but right then, I couldn't help but feel it. They sized me up, glancing at me, not in a bad way, more like they were trying to figure out how to be around me. They were overly polite, like they were stepping on eggshells. It wasn't anything new, though. I knew, even then, that this stage didn't last long. Soon enough, they would get used to me.

They picked out the smallest seat they had. Once it was bolted in place, I slid into position as they wedged foam inserts tightly around me, packing the gaps between my frame and the seat. It wasn't ideal, they said, but it would have to do. As I was strapped in, I shifted slightly, testing the fit – no give, no slack, just firm, locked in. Perfect.

The mechanic leaned in and asked if I wanted padding on each side of my head. It was a genuine offer to take the stress off my neck. But I knew how this worked – none of the male drivers ever took the padding. Refusing it was an unspoken ritual, a declaration that your neck was strong enough to take the strain. It wasn't about comfort; it was about proving you could handle it. So, I said no. If they didn't need it, neither did I.

I sat in the car, waiting for the signal to exit the garage. Having tested the car before, I knew what to expect, and I remembered I'd loved driving it. That familiarity gave me confidence. Mika's notes played out in my mind – the racing lines, the braking points, the gear shifts. The engineer waved me forward. Let's go.

After a few laps it was time to push, to find the pace. I didn't dive in headfirst, guns blazing like some young, hot-blooded male drivers. I built speed brick by brick, lap by lap. Comfort isn't speed – I knew that. I braked harder, later, inching closer to the limit. That felt too easy. *Go later*, I said to myself. But I pushed too far, locked up and missed the apex. The margin narrowed, and I began to feel the tightrope I must walk – the fine line.

But then, something was wrong. The car pulled left under braking, subtle but unmistakable. If it was a puncture, I'd have felt it now, but the car stayed planted. I braked again, and there it was – a sharp pull, unsettling, like an invisible hand tugging the wheel as I squeezed down on the brakes.

I pulled into the garage, and Gerhard appeared.

How's it going out there?

It's okay but something isn't right, the car keeps pulling to the left, under braking.

He turned to the engineer, and suddenly, they were deep in a rapid-fire exchange of German. I couldn't catch a single word. Gerhard called someone else over. As the person came into view it dawned on me, I had seen that race suit before. I recognised that name. Bernd Schneider. *The* Bernd Schneider. A four-time DTM champion. Just months ago, I'd shoved his racing suit back into a cardboard box, completely unaware of who he was.

Gerhard gestured for him to test the car. My seat was pulled from the cockpit, Bernd's was bolted in, and within moments, he was climbing into the car. As I stood there watching, doubt started creeping in. Were they questioning my feedback? Did they think the problem wasn't the car but me? I could only hope Bernd would feel what I had felt – because otherwise, this was going to be humiliating.

After three laps, the car returned to the pits. Bernd climbed out, exchanged a few words with Gerhard and cast a glance in my direction. Gerhard's expression shifted as he relayed the verdict: there was indeed an issue with the front brakes. Phew. What a relief. The mechanics replaced the brake discs, and soon I was back on track.

The improvement was instant, and with a renewed sense of confidence, I started to build, attacking harder. Lap by lap, I was improving. The dashboard; displayed a glowing LED '–' or '+', a silent *pollice verso* passing judgement – quicker or slower. But what was the benchmark? How did I measure up against the other drivers? I had no idea. Back in the garage, they remained as stony-faced as ever – no pats on the back, no words of encouragement, just the constant low hum of German conversations I couldn't follow.

By the time the midday break was called, I stepped out of the garage to grab my jacket from the truck. I was aware I was being watched by an older man, balding head and with a huge belly pulling at the buttons of his Mercedes shirt. He sauntered over to me, a cigarette dangling from his lips.

I'm Doc Schmidt. I'm the team doctor. A doctor? He was hardly an advert for healthy living.

You're doing well. Keep it up.

This small comment, such simple words, meant so much in that moment.

Thank you, Doc.

Everyone around me had these unreadable poker faces. I'd pretty much accepted I'd be in the dark the whole test. But then Doc had given me a quiet vote of confidence, like maybe, just maybe, I was actually on the right track.

After lunch, I was back in the car. The engineer's feedback nudged me towards small improvements. I felt myself adapting to the characteristics of the car, settling into a rhythm. I'd come in, we'd discuss setup changes, and then I'd head back out. Each time the '–' glowed on my dashboard; I was steadily getting quicker. That feeling when you're on form and everything's clicking – the adrenaline kicking in, like being in a state of pure flow and my senses operating on another level – razor-sharp, dialled in.

Then before I knew it, the test was over. As I changed and prepared to leave, I made it a point to thank everyone – the engineers, the mechanics, everyone I had met that day. My final stop was Gerhard. I expressed my gratitude for the opportunity and asked if there was any feedback.

We'll be in touch.

Okay. Thank you. I went in for another stab. *But was there anything I could improve on?*

We'll be in touch.

This time, he spaced out the words evenly, drawing a line under the conversation. I took this as my cue to leave. I glanced over at Doc Schmidt, who gave me a small wink. Was this a glimmer of hope?

*   *   *

Back in Northampton, I didn't let my phone out of my sight, checking it constantly to ensure I always had signal and enough battery. Days soon turned into a week. Desperation began to creep in. Had I done enough? Had my growing confidence been misplaced? This was all I had left – my last lifeline.

After ten days, the +49 German number finally flashed up on my phone. Elation. The voice on the other end was calm and direct, asking if it was me. I confirmed. They asked me to hold the line, and then came the voice I'd been desperate to hear: Gerhard Ungar. He told me to get to Stuttgart the next day for a meeting.

A driver met me at the airport and dropped me off at the Mercedes-Benz headquarters. Inside, I was directed to a sleek waiting area. The walls were lined with posters in muted greys and silvers, each showcasing their latest models. I sat down and rehearsed some German lines I had in my head.

Ich freue mich, hier zu sein. I'm happy to be here.

Hours passed – two, then three, then four. I began to wonder if they'd forgotten about me. But I was here now, and I wasn't going anywhere. Finally, a young woman appeared and motioned for me to follow. I was led upstairs to the fifth floor, and everything changed. This was clearly the motorsport floor. The sterile corporate grey gave way to vibrant colours, the space pulsing with life. Trophies lined glass cases, each one holding its own story of triumph. The walls were covered in bold images of racing moments, spanning decades and show-casing Mercedes-Benz's legacy in motorsport – this was the heart of their racing division. This was where it all happened. Representing Mercedes-Benz in Formula One that year, McLaren-Mercedes had Kimi Räikkönen and Juan Pablo Montoya, their neon orange Vodafone livery cutting through the signature silver.

I followed the woman through a maze of corridors until she opened the door to a massive boardroom. At the head of the table sat Norbert Haug, head of Mercedes-Benz Motorsport, with Gerhard to his left. I extended my hand and said, *Guten Tag. Ich freue mich sehr, hier zu sein.* [*Hello, I'm very happy to be here.*]

Norbert raised an eyebrow. *Sie können Deutsch sprechen?* [*You can speak German?*]

Ja, ein bisschen. Ich habe es in der Schule gelernt. [*Yes, a little. I studied it in school.*]

A faint smile crossed his face.

Norbert didn't waste time. Leaning forward, he got straight to the point. He laid out the offer plainly: a one-year deal to drive for Mercedes-Benz in the DTM. This was it. The moment I had dreamed of, held onto in the months of despair, the chance I had been so desperate for. They saw my face light up.

Danke. Danke. Danke.

Gerhard then said my car would benefit from a 20-kilogram weight reduction to ensure I would be competitive. What?

I don't need a weight advantage. Before I could catch myself, the words were out.

The room fell silent.

Norbert sized me up, his expression unreadable, while Gerhard remained motionless. I wondered if I'd overstepped, but I had never needed an unfair advantage to compete and I wasn't going to start now. After a long moment, Norbert nodded.

Fine. You'll be the same weight.

Thank you.

Norbert extended his hand.

Welcome to the Mercedes-Benz family.

Stepping out of the boardroom, my heart was pounding in my chest. The words *Welcome to the Mercedes-Benz family* played over and over in my mind. Before I reached the car waiting to take me back to the airport, I pulled out my phone and dialled home.

Mum, Dad. We've done it. I'm a Mercedes DTM driver.

Mum screamed with joy. Dad tried to speak, I could hear him choking up. This wasn't just my win – it was ours. We'd been through every obstacle together, every crushing disappointment, every moment of doubt.

From that moment on, life became a whirlwind. Within days, my email inbox was flooded – contracts, details for testing schedules, helmet sticker requirements, uniform sizes, and an endless list of preparations for the season ahead.

A week later, a large box arrived at my house in Northampton. Inside was my official Mercedes-Benz team kit. Piece by piece, I unpacked it, each item emblazoned with the iconic Mercedes star. There was training gear, casual wear and, of course, my race suit – each item immaculate, my name stitched into the fabric. It felt like a declaration: I'm now a professional racing driver. I spread everything out carefully, obsessively folding and organising it.

And then, a brand-new Mercedes-AMG C 63 showed up in the driveway – I couldn't stop staring at it. I'd sit inside, fire up the engine, and just hear that growl. Every morning, I'd check outside the window first thing, and every night before bed, I'd look again, just to make sure it was still there – that this was all real.

The final piece of this new reality clicked into place when the first payment from Mercedes landed in my bank account. I jumped into my new car and drove straight to the nearest ATM – not to withdraw cash but just to see the number on the screen. I'd never seen a balance like that before.

I was twenty-three, and life had transformed dramatically, but I was ready for it. I couldn't wait to get racing.

9

THE first stop was a four-day pre-season test in Estoril, Portugal. I was taken to meet the engineer who would be running me, Hans Peter, known as HP. Big, burly and bald but instantly friendly. HP got straight to the point. As we sat down for our first meeting, he laid out the reality with a directness that set the tone for what was to come.

You haven't raced for a year. No Formula Three experience. The level up will shock you.

Shock me? Of course it would. Every step up in motorsport is a shock, a jolt to the system. I knew that now. And I would manage this the only way I knew: preparation and attention to detail.

I soon realised that HP was also a details guy, and we immediately clicked. He spent the first few hours making sure I understood every aspect of what was ahead. From the dynamics between teams to the key players and the structure of each day, he broke it all down for me. I discovered I'd be racing an older spec car. HP explained that these weren't in contention for the championship. My battle would be all in midfield, and that was if we were doing well. The goalposts had moved, but I rationalised that if I could do a good job, the possibility of driving the new spec championship fighting cars would be on the cards.

The first day of testing was all about qualifying. I'd never seen so many sets of new tyres in my life. Growing up, tyres were a luxury – every new set had to be budgeted for. But here, new tyres were always on hand, with no hesitation, no consideration of cost. The focus was clear: prepare the tyres on the out-lap, push hard on the first lap, cool them down, and go again. It was all about finding the limit, discovering the absolute fastest point you could push to.

On the second day, we shifted to race starts and pit stops. DTM's hour-long races with two pit stops were a whole new concept for me. In my single-seater racing, I had never done a pit stop. I had to learn to stop the car with millimetre precision – stopping outside the box even slightly could delay the mechanics. Then, how to leave the pit stop cleanly, avoiding wheelspin but also not stalling.

Day three was race simulations. These mimic the full race distances, pushing both the car and the driver throughout the day. Over 120 laps, they tested endurance as much as performance. By mid-afternoon, Estoril's long, flat-out right-hander proved to be my breaking point. My neck gave up. I had to prop my head against my shoulder, the only way to make it through the corner.

When the day finally ended, I drove back to the hotel, utterly shattered. As soon as I walked in, I went straight to reception and asked for some ice – lots of it. When they returned with a small champagne bucket of ice, I shook my head and pleaded.

I need more, a lot more, please.

Eventually, a massive plastic bag of ice was delivered, and I collapsed face down on the bed, resting the bag on my neck and back, letting the chill seep into my battered muscles.

The next morning, I tried to lift my head but simply couldn't – it had seized tight through the night. The only option was to roll out of bed, landing in a graceless sprawl on the floor. Crawling into the shower, I cranked the water to the highest temperature I could tolerate. I pressed my fingers into the stiff cords of muscle along my neck and up to the base of my skull. Slowly, I massaged and stretched, coaxing the tension to release. Each tiny bit of movement felt like progress, but the thought of getting back into the car made me wince.

When I got to the track, I told HP about my neck. Without hesitation, he got to work with the mechanics, building in two small foam pads in the headrest that I could rest my neck against. The bravado I had clung to in the first test, insisting I didn't need any padding, crumbled. At that point, I needed all the help I could get just to make it through. I reasoned with myself that I'd ditch them as soon as the strength in my neck came back. My hands, raw and blistered from gripping the steering wheel, were another problem. HP taped them up like a boxer preparing for a fight.

The heat was also beginning to take its toll – being in the car for long stretches was suffocating, like sitting in an oven. There was a small air vent, but no one ever used it. The logic? Any air pulled into the car would slow it down. That's just how it was. Over the course of the test, I'd done nearly 300 laps and with that, more than 9,000 gear shifts – each one like a single-arm row at the gym. My arms burned, my body ached, and the heat just kept building, layer upon layer.

I focused on just trying to keep my lap times consistent – managing the tyre degradation, a key element in any race. We entered the final stint: ten laps. *One lap at a time*, I told myself. *Just get through it.* When the pit board finally showed 'L1' – last lap – I thought, *Thank goodness.* I couldn't wait for it to be over.

HP came over the radio. *Lap times are really consistent.*

I thought, *You've done it, Susie. Just one more lap.*

Then I heard him say, *Let's go for another ten.*

I could've cried. I most definitely swore. Ten more laps.

OK. Deep breath. I tried again:

One good lap. Then another. And another.

The test finished and I was wiped out, just relieved it was over.

I was then told to pack quickly – all drivers would be flying with Mika in his private jet to the fitness week. A private jet? Wow. I didn't want to look like the rookie I was or seem too impressed, but it was my first time on a private jet. I had only ever flown economy class. This was a glimpse into a lifestyle I hadn't even known existed.

The flight itself was short, just twenty minutes, and I barely had time to soak in the moment before we were already descending. Cars met us on arrival and we were whisked up winding roads to a stunning mountain retreat: a golf resort near Faro in the Algarve. The rolling green hills, manicured grounds and luxurious hotel felt like a respite from the hard days I had just endured – or so I thought.

That evening, as we sat down for dinner, I got my first look at the programme for the week. If I had imagined this was going to be a chance to recover, I was sorely mistaken. Toni Mathis, the team trainer, was older and Austrian, with a strong muscular build that left no doubt about his own fitness.

Okay, the programme has been designed for the boys. You were a late addition. We'll figure out something different for you.

I wasn't about to let that slide.

I'm driving the same car, Toni. I need to do the same programme.

He looked at me, taken aback, but after a moment, he nodded.

Okay then. Let's give it a try.

The week kicked off with a mountain hike early the next morning. The schedule hadn't left much to the imagination: 'Mountain Climb', it had said in big bold letters. I stood there, staring up at the climb ahead, and realised it was going to be even harder than I'd first thought. I knew the science, women have 30 per cent less muscle than men, I was disadvantaged in pure power, but so what? That wasn't an excuse I could use in a race, and it wasn't one I'd let myself use now.

I joined the others as we assembled at the base of the mountain. Everything is a competition with racing drivers but as we set off, it was clear that this was going to be a battle with myself rather than with the others. The climb was unrelenting and unforgiving. My lungs burned, my heart pounded, and the heat in my face made me feel like I was about to ignite. I didn't even want to look at the reading on my heart rate monitor. But I refused to stop. The group ahead would pause every so often, taking short breaks, glancing back to check on me, lagging but still climbing, always climbing. Their pace was something I couldn't match, but I wouldn't let myself rest. Step by step, I kept moving.

By the time we were three-quarters of the way up my legs felt like lead, and every step was a fight against the urge to give in. Then I saw them, huddled together, waiting. When I finally caught up, Toni clapped me on the back with a wide grin and said, *Now we go to the top. All together.*

They had watched me struggle, but they also saw that I hadn't quit. We reached the summit together, I was part of the pack. Something shifted that day. They understood I wasn't there for special treatment, and I never expected it. I wasn't trying to make a statement or demand space – I was simply earning my place. And in doing so, I felt I had earned their respect.

The next morning, we moved to the pool. I knew the moment I saw it on the programme – this would be my revenge. I had always kept up my swimming; it had remained a steady part of my training. My teammates arrived in long, loose-fitting board shorts. *First mistake*, I thought, *they are just going to slow you down.* Toni told us to do a few lengths to warm up. As the others fumbled with their goggles and nonchalantly made their way to the edge of the pool, I dived in and started a gentle warm-up. At each end of the pool, I did a tumble turn until I was aware I was still the only one in the water. Stopping, I saw everyone still on the edge of the pool, looking down at me.

One of them blurted out, *So you can swim.* The surprise was plain in his voice.

I laughed. *I can swim.*

Toni revelled at the tables being turned. *So we've got a swimmer among us, boys!*

By the end of the week, I was no longer just the girl on the team. I was one of them, and in the pool, I'd shown them exactly what I was made of. The jokes about girls, the kind they might've thought would irritate me before, started to flow more freely – but this time, I laughed with them. I understood it was their way of bonding.

All week, I had welcomed the searing pain I'd put my body through. Now, I could feel it working: torn muscle fibres were growing back stronger. I imagined them growing thicker, a dense weave: a fibrous armour.

Not long after, I was booked to go to Stuttgart for an official photoshoot. It was during this shoot that I met Mathias Lauda for the first time. As the son of Niki Lauda, his name carried an immense legacy. Niki Lauda, one of Formula One's greatest drivers, was a legend, and Mathias was now forging his own path in motorsport. Mathias and I instantly warmed to each other as we shared the same sense of humour. We were both new to the Mercedes team, both acutely aware of the immense task ahead. Our teammates were blisteringly fast, and the bar couldn't have been set higher.

Following the photoshoot came the official announcement: I was now a Mercedes-Benz works driver. On 24 February 2006, everything changed. My name was suddenly out there, tied to one of the most prestigious car manufacturers in the world. Overnight, I went from being just another driver trying to make my mark to representing the silver star. With that came a whole new level of expectation – and visibility.

Straight after the announcement, I headed to Düsseldorf for the championship presentation. I'd never been to Düsseldorf before and hadn't spent much time in Germany beyond passing through on the way to kart races. I didn't know what to expect – how big it would be, or even what a 'presentation' entailed. But the moment I arrived, the sheer scale of it all hit me.

We were put up in the best hotel. Stepping to the window, I looked out to see the streets cornered off, lined with DTM signs, my face plastered on posters, and crowds gathered everywhere. That was when it hit me: *Oh my God, this is big*.

For the first time in my career, I had my own autograph cards. Of course, I'd been asked for the odd autograph back in my Formula Renault days, but this was on a completely different scale. There I was, signing stacks of cards for fans. This wasn't small-time anymore – this was the big league.

My other teammates were Mika Häkkinen, already a legend with two Formula One World Championships to his name; Jean Alesi, a former Ferrari F1 driver; Bernd Schneider, one of DTM's biggest stars; Jamie Green, a young British driver and former Formula Three European Champion who was hotly tipped for a future in Formula One; and Bruno Spengler, a fast young Canadian. The level of talent around me was staggering, and it brought home just how high the bar was set.

Then it was on to the first round of the DTM season, at Hockenheim. Close to 120,000 people attended, and the race would be broadcast all over Europe. The crowds had been building all weekend – many camping overnight, creating a carnival-like atmosphere unique to DTM. The German public adored it: German cars battling for dominance. I had never seen full grandstands or a paddock swarming with fans asking for autographs and photos before. That's the magic of DTM – fans aren't just spectators, they're part of the experience, mingling freely and connecting with the drivers. The walkways to the garages had to be cordoned off to manage the crowds. This was motorsport on a scale I had never experienced – intense and surreal. I had to pinch myself just to believe I was really part of it. I loved every moment.

TV crews were everywhere. I was so focused on my schedule that there was no time to feel overwhelmed. Every minute of my day was accounted for, from heading to the stage for interviews to media sessions, engineering briefings, pre-race strategy meetings and debriefs after each session. Even break times were carefully planned – I could decide whether to rest in the truck or head to hospitality where my meals were already prepared. For someone who valued order and preparation, I thrived in such a structured environment.

Race day brought an entirely new level of anticipation. Traffic jammed the roads leading to the circuit. Fans lined up everywhere, even watching as I parked my car.

Mathias Lauda had mentioned earlier in the weekend that his father, Niki, would be coming to watch him race for the first time. Niki Lauda, the three-time Formula One World Champion and the face of Formula One commentary on Germany's biggest TV network. His presence in the paddock was an event in itself. The moment he stepped into our garage, the energy shifted – the atmosphere bristled with anticipation.

We were lined up to greet him, Mathias standing beside me. Niki entered with his trademark briskness, giving the team a quick nod before stopping in front of his son. Niki cast me a brief glance, then turned to Mathias.

The most important thing. Beat her.

Mathias glanced at me, rolling his eyes as if to say sorry. Niki, completely unfazed, didn't bother to shake my hand or speak to me. He just walked away, leaving me standing there. That moment stayed with me. Usually, I let things slide – but if there's one thing that gets under my skin, it's being dismissed.

Years later, I reminded Niki of it, recounting how rude he had been. He didn't deny it.

You're right, he admitted. *That really wasn't nice. And I'm sorry. But I didn't know you were going to be quick.*

As the race approached, Mathias and I climbed into the back of an open-top car for the parade lap. Waving Mercedes flags, we were driven around the circuit as the grandstands erupted with cheers. After the lap, I returned to my car. I'm someone who likes to get in early – I have this recurring nightmare of a race starting without me, my helmet not fastened up or my gloves not on. Strapping in early helped calm those nerves. My spot on the grid was marked by a pit girl in a bright yellow Deutsche Post outfit, holding a board with my name on it. It was a racing tradition and I didn't give it a second thought. My focus was elsewhere – getting everything ready for the race.

At ten minutes to go, the countdown began.

Inside the car, I did a radio check, and my engineer reminded me of the key things I needed to focus on: tyre temperatures, practice starts to get heat into the clutch, and making sure I nailed the launch off the line. As much as you try to visualise it, the start is always instinctive – decisions are made in a split second as you see how everything unfolds on the track.

I saw the big boss, Norbert Haug, approaching my car. He leaned in and clasped my hand.

Have a good race – and on the formation lap, look up at the Mercedes-Benz grandstand.

At the five-minute mark, the tyres were mounted onto the car and the crew began to disappear.

At one minute, the door shut. It was the point of no return – just me, the car and the race ahead.

Clockwise, from top left: Mum on her quad bike; with my brother David at a quad race; my first 3-wheeler quad bike, which I got for Christmas; on the *Funhouse* kart track; on my PW80, trying to keep up with Mum and David; my first kart race with our little tow-a-van.

Above, clockwise from top left: The early pink race suit; European Championships with Peter de Bruijn racing; Lotta Hellberg, who I looked up to; Formula Renault Brands Hatch.

Left: On the Formula Renault podium with Lewis.

This cartoon summed up the Autosport Young Driver of the Year Award in 2003 . . .

Bamber's VIEW

THE WINNER OF THE McLAREN AUTOSPORT BRDC TROPHY WILL BE ANNOUNCED AT THE END OF THE EVENING — SO SEE YOU LATER **LADS!**

WHAT?

AUTOSPORT
Autosport awards 2003
GROSVENOR HOTEL

THE MOMENT SUSIE STODDART KNEW SHE HAD NO CHANCE!

We made it! With Mum and Dad in DTM.

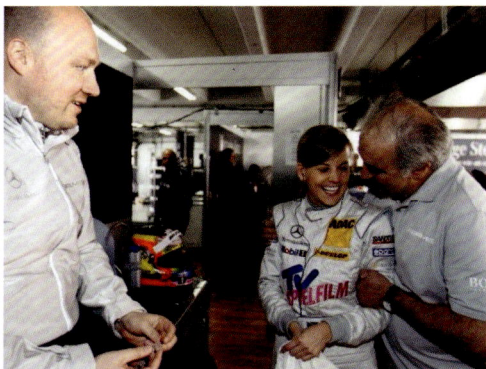
With my engineer HP and Doc Schmidt.

The pink car.

Strapped in and ready to go.

With my Mercedes DTM teammates.

The Mercedes Benz Grandstand at my first race.

With Toto.

Walking through Capri after the church ceremony on our wedding day.

Above left: Waiting for my first ever outing in the Williams F1 car at Silverstone.

Above right: Now the team's test driver and ready to go.

Right: Disbelief when my engine stopped on the first lap at the British GP practice session.

Left: On Channel 4's F1 coverage with Toto and David Coulthard.

Rosi and Bene.

Jack.

With Gildo Pastor and Felipe Massa in Monaco.

On the Formula E podium to collect the team trophy.

The whole ROKiT Venturi Formula E Team celebrating a victory together.

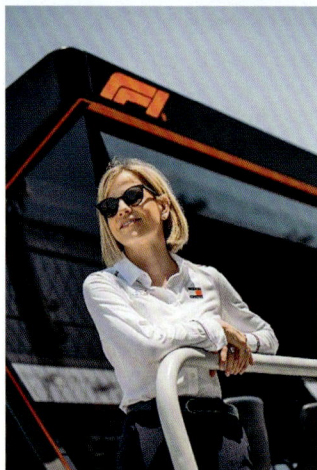

Clockwise, from top left: with Toto and Jack; celebrating an F1 win with Toto; on the F1 pitwall; with Derek Chang, Bruno Michel, Stefano Domenicali and Chase Carey on the F1 Academy grid in Jeddah; with Lewis at the first F1 Academy race alongside F1; on the pitwall with Delphine, Head of Race Operations at F1 Academy.

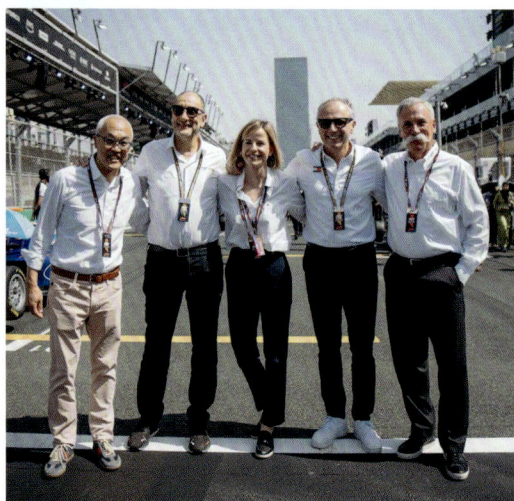

As I set off on the green flag lap, warming the brakes and fine-tuning the temperatures, the Mercedes-Benz grandstand came into view. Just as Norbert had told me, I looked up – and there it was. All 12,000 spectators holding up coloured placards, perfectly arranged to spell 'HELLO SUSIE', with the Scottish flag above. A sight so surreal, it momentarily cut through the intense focus of the moment.

Oh. My. Goodness. I couldn't even register what I was seeing.

Susie – don't think about that now – focus.

My engineer guided me over the radio into my exact position – *Go, go, go, stop!* – to make sure I was perfectly aligned in my box.

The marshal at the back waved the green flag, and the light sequence began. My heart pounded. Time slowed. Nothing else existed – just the lights, each one flicking on.

One, two, three, four, five . . .

My clutch hovered at the bite point, my revs steady at the golden number – 30 per cent throttle. The lights went out.

GO.

I launched off the line, making a clean start. The cars in front of me fanned out, three, four, five abreast.

I immediately moved to the outside, avoiding a slower car that had caused a bottleneck into the first corner. Swinging wide, I regained track position and was alongside the Audi of Christian Abt who was sponsored by *Playboy*, with its iconic black livery and white bunny. We were side by side, muscling each other for track position. I held the inside but he didn't give an inch on the exit and suddenly we were three abreast, engines screaming in unison. I held my ground on the inside line and edged ahead – he then clipped the other car. The corner erupted in chaos – screeching tyres, smoke, and the white bunny was in a spin. Two more places gained.

By the time I crossed the line at the end of the lap and saw my pit board, I was up to P14. The next lap, coming into the long hairpin three cars went side by side into the corner. I saw the opportunity, diving to the inside. As they tangled, one car's rear bumper flew off, and I exited cleanly, gaining two positions to P12. Jean Alesi, directly behind me, started to pull out along the straights as if to say – I'm here and I'm coming past. I glanced in my mirrors, and ignored him. I wasn't going to let him rattle me into a mistake, then, under braking, I felt a tap from behind, hard enough to unsettle my car and force me wide. Jean glided past up my inside. I made a mental note: so, that's how we race here.

Six laps in, pit stops began. Cars ahead peeled off, and suddenly, I was in P6. The laps between pit stops were critical – every second mattered. When my time came on lap 27, I hit my marks perfectly. The team's lollipop man guided me into position and the tyres were changed in under six seconds. The car thudded back onto the ground, and I nailed the exit, avoiding wheelspin as I drifted back into the fast lane.

Back on track, I was battling for position again. I'd dropped back to P12 but had fresher tyres than most of the field. It was all about managing the rubber, avoiding overheating and letting the grip come to me. With twelve laps to go, I locked onto my next target, speeding down the straight at 280kph, closing the gap, when suddenly, chaos erupted. Sparks flew. Smoke billowed. An Audi car fighting for a podium had shredded his front tyre. At that speed, reactions had to be instinctive. I barely had time to process it before I was ploughing through the haze, vision obscured for a split second.

Nine laps remained, and I was one of the only cars yet to make my second pit stop. The team finally called me in. As I exited the pit lane, I found myself back in P12. Now, it was a fight to the finish. With fresher tyres, I clawed back two positions. The race ended with fireworks lighting up the circuit. Bernd Schneider took the win. I crossed the line in P10, only forty-four seconds behind the leader after an hour of racing and two pit stops.

Back in the garage, my engineer was laughing with my mechanics. As I joined them he said, *Listen to this, Susie. Two laps into the race, Jean Alesi came over the radio and said, 'Get this girl out of my way.'*

I smiled, but my engineer wasn't finished.

He continued, *No one knew what to say to him. But then Jean came back, shouting, 'I told you to get this girl out of my way!' Finally, his engineer replied, 'Jean, we can't. You'll have to race her.'*

I laughed. Jean Alesi – a former Ferrari driver, no less – had been rattled enough to call me out mid-race. That moment set the tone for my early relationship with him. At the beginning we were never close. Jean was fiery, ego-driven, the classic alpha male. A former F1 star, he wasn't used to facing someone like me. But I didn't care – I wasn't there for his approval. Still, as with many of my teammates, mutual respect developed over time.

After the race, as I was packing up my helmet and suit I was summoned to a meeting with Norbert and Hans Werner Aufrecht, the founder and the 'A' of AMG. One of the most respected and feared names in the paddock who I had only seen from a distance, he was known for being very tough, especially with drivers.

I stepped into the private, cordoned-off area of the hospitality suite where the two men were sitting on large leather chairs, cigars in hand. Hans Werner, in his heavy German accent, spoke first.

Strong first race, he said simply.

Norbert leaned forward, smiling. *You have the chance to make a great career with us*, he said, *but I'll give you one piece of advice: learn German, and learn it fast.*

I heard his message loud and clear. If I wanted to integrate into the team and the culture fully, I needed to speak the language.

The Monday morning after the race, back in Northampton, I wasted no time finding a German tutor. I called my parents, asking them to send all my old German notes from school, and booked a set of two-hour lessons three times a week.

I told my tutor to focus on racing terms first. I didn't care about ordering coffee or asking for directions to the train station. What mattered was being able to say *My start was good*, or *The car felt quick*. It was like being back in school, but I had the basics thanks to Dad's guidance to pick German over French in high school. I started making progress quickly and within a few months I was doing basic interviews in German.

I soon learned that a highlight of DTM was the mid-season race through the streets of Nuremberg, known as the Norisring, a tight and punishing street circuit that carves its way through the heart of a historic setting. The track runs along the stone grandstands of the infamous Nazi rally grounds. It's one of the few street circuits on the calendar – short, brutally bumpy and, at seventy-four laps, relentlessly physical. And from the first lap, I loved it. No runoff areas, no room for mistakes – just you and the walls.

As my grasp of the language improved, I found myself integrating more naturally into the team. Each evening during race weekends, Mercedes designated a central table in the hospitality area where all the drivers would gather for dinner. I was chatting with Mathias Lauda, who sat across from me, when I noticed a man walk in.

I didn't know who he was but he had a certain aura about him. He was tall, dark and incredibly handsome. He moved from table to table, talking to people, and I found myself completely distracted watching him. Mathias noticed, turning to see what – or who – had caught my attention.

When he turned back, he said, *Susie, you're looking at him.*

I immediately flushed red, caught off guard.

You like him, Mathias said, grinning as he leaned back in his chair.

Who is he? I asked.

Mathias smirked.

He's Austrian. Works in finance. His name's Toto Wolff. And . . . he added with a dramatic pause, *You have absolutely no chance. He's dating Miss Austria.*

The next day, I was having a strong run. Two-thirds into the race, I was sitting in tenth and feeling good. A year-old car meant I wasn't getting all the latest upgrades, so fighting at the front was out of the question. But being the best of the rest? That was still on the table.

With eight laps to go, I was in a long train of cars, pushing hard.

Then, the first hairpin.

It's a tight, 180-degree corner, the slowest part of the track. I turned in, ready to power out, when – bang.

Impact.

A massive hit from the side. No warning. No time to brace. The force was so big it knocked the wind straight out of me. Being a left-hand-drive car, the impact was on my side.

I didn't even process who hit me at first. Later, I found out that a car running in P12 had lost its brakes. This track is notorious for it. The heavy braking zones, the relentless heat – it cooks the brake discs. Managing them is everything. But his were completely gone, and he flew straight into me. I sat in the wreck, trying to gulp for air. The paramedic yanked the door open. I wasn't injured, I just couldn't breathe. The impact had knocked every bit of air out of my lungs.

Are you okay?

No words came out. I nodded my head, pointing to my chest.

The paramedic panicked.

Before I could even catch enough breath to tell him I was fine, they had a needle in my arm, delivering a shot of sedative as they thought I was in shock.

And just like that, I went limp.

I remember feeling weightless, my body slack, my mind fully aware but disconnected from my legs and arms. They pulled me from the car and loaded me into the ambulance. Again, I tried to speak, to tell them I was all right, but my mouth wouldn't move.

At the hospital, the tests all came back clear. By evening, I was back at the track. Everyone kept asking – *Are you okay?* But I could still only slur; if you didn't know what had happened, you'd think I was drunk. It wasn't a good look. It took a full twenty-four hours for the sedative to wear off but that hardly mattered to me: I was more frustrated at the unfortunate loss of a top-ten finish.

Towards the end of that first season, I was offered a new three-year contract. For the first time, I had stability and financial security. I no longer worried about finding the budget to race or lived with the constant unease of whether my racing would continue. It felt like a huge weight had lifted. On the way to race weekends, I often found myself reflecting, grateful that a single test in Barcelona had changed not only the course of my career but my life.

Then came the legal letter. I found out that, due to financial difficulties, Paul, my manager, had transferred my management contract to a business associate. I was suddenly caught in the middle of something I hadn't seen coming. What followed was a blur of legal calls and negotiations – exhausting, disorienting, and completely beyond me. I hated every moment of it. I wanted to be in control, but instead, I found myself reacting to decisions I hadn't been part of.

At a Mercedes event, Mika and his manager, Didier Coton, quickly picked up on my distress. Call after call, I was pulled away, each one more frantic than the last. They were far more versed in dealing with such legal minefields and stepped in to help me untangle the situation. After a tense back-and-forth with lawyers, we finally reached a resolution. I acknowledged the role Paul had played in helping me – but now, I was free. I didn't seek new management; I felt ready to handle my own affairs.

Once the stress was over I had clarity about exactly what I needed to do next, an absolute belief in my own abilities, and I didn't feel afraid: I knew what I needed to be successful, and I understood that in an environment as tough and unforgiving as DTM, I intended to fight for it. I sat down and wrote a letter to Norbert Haug and Gerhard Ungar. By then, I had started to understand the environment and knew what, and who, I needed to give me a better chance of getting closer to the front – a stronger team. It was, without a doubt, a very ballsy move, but by that point I had grown accustomed to the direct German way of communicating and wanted them to know I was capable of more.

I never received a reply. Instead, just a few weeks later, I was informed that I would be switching teams and engineers for the following season, exactly as I had asked for.

10

THAT winter, I made the decision to move to Switzerland, on the German border. I would be closer to the Mercedes HQ, my team, and most importantly, I wanted to immerse myself and become fluent in German. During my last lesson in Northampton, my tutor told me I would be fluent in three months, but this seemed unrealistic given my inability to even hold a conversation thus far, despite many hours with him.

Living in Switzerland was like stepping onto another planet. I rented a small apartment on Lake Constance, a place that reminded me of home because of the water. Everything else was completely foreign. No one spoke English or even attempted to, so I carried a small German dictionary everywhere. Even the simplest tasks, like following road signs or posting a letter, became challenges that left me mentally fatigued. By the end of each day, I wouldn't even want to switch the TV on, but rather relish the silence to give my brain a rest. Gradually it got easier and without even realising it was happening, the conversations in German started to flow. My tutor hadn't been wrong – within three months, I was nearly fluent. It transformed my race weekends: I could follow conversations in the garage and give interviews in German. My grammatical slip-ups often sparked laughter, but it was at least clear to everyone that I'd made a real effort.

I was starting to find my feet, settling into myself, but at the same time, I was being confronted – over and over again – with my own image, and I didn't like what I saw. The suit I was wearing on last year's autograph card from the previous season made me look bulky. Every time I signed a card, I had to face the image again and again. So this year, I decided to take control. I had the pockets removed from my suit, the belt cinched in. I had my team clothing tailored to fit properly. Clean lines, sharper silhouette.

It was a constant question, a quiet tug-of-war within me – what did my clothing say about me? What message was I sending? On one hand, I wanted to be seen first and foremost as a racing driver. When I took off my helmet, I resisted the instinct to fix my sweat-dampened hair, unwilling to give anyone the impression that vanity ranked higher than performance. Eventually, my engineer, nudged by the marketing department, would hand me a team cap – an unspoken compromise.

As my calendar filled with events alongside my race weekends, I was scheduled for a visit to Hugo Boss, the manufacturer of our team kit and a key sponsor of Mercedes-Benz in both DTM and Formula One. All drivers wore Hugo Boss suits, and I was there to be fitted for my own. The factory, located not far from the Mercedes-Benz headquarters in

Stuttgart, had an air of sleek efficiency. As I arrived, Lewis Hamilton's McLaren-Mercedes Formula One car stood on display near the entrance – a reminder of just how far we had come in the sport from those early karting days. Till Pohlmann, the head of sponsorship, greeted me and led me into the factory shop, an expansive industrial-style warehouse lined with endless racks of clothing.

Take your time, he said, before stepping away. *If you need anything, ask one of the assistants.*

I wandered through the aisles, overwhelmed by the sheer volume – suits, dresses, coats, all impeccably tailored. I imagined all the outfits for the events in my calendar, but every time I turned over a price tag, I silently baulked. A coat was €800. A suit, €700. At that point, I'd only recently cleared my debts, paying back loans taken out to fund my racing, and I was just out of my first season with a contract. Spending that kind of money on clothes felt like too much too soon.

After about an hour, I found a fitted trouser suit. Practical, versatile and it could be dressed up or down, plus not too expensive. When Till came back, he looked at the lone trouser suit on the rack and asked, *Is that it?*

Yes. I think this is all I need, thank you.

He paused and an awkward silence ensued.

You know you don't have to pay for any of this, right?

Right. No, I didn't realise that.

Really? That is very kind.

You should take another look.

Okay, I will. Thank you.

Take this rail and load it up.

I could hardly believe my luck. The young girl in me, the one who used to help out in my mum's shop, watching in wonder as outfits came together, had returned. Only this time, it was my turn. For the next three hours, I lost myself in the joy of it: carefully selecting coats, dresses, suits and shoes, assembling looks piece by piece.

When I got home, I savoured the unwrapping of each item. My wardrobe had suddenly quadrupled in size, and I felt an exhilaration, as if I was now stepping into a new version of myself. For the first time, I had options, real options. Every outfit decision beyond my team kit or race suit became a conscious choice. What did I want my clothes to say about me?

I didn't want to appear as though I was dressing to grab attention. But I also wasn't prepared to fade into the background. The focus had to remain on my ability, not my appearance. I'd always been mindful of that. Still, I was feminine. I loved fashion. And now, with access to beautiful clothes, I finally had the freedom to show that part of myself.

As the 2007 season progressed, I started to understand not just how I was perceived but also where I sat within the dynamics of the grid. My image wasn't just about me anymore – it was becoming a tool in the marketing machine. That awareness came into sharp focus when Audi signed a female driver and there was a push to frame us as rivals. The DTM organisers proposed a photoshoot: just the two of us as if we were boxers squaring off in a ring.

I hated the idea. The narrative was reductive – two women, racing only against each other, as if the rest of the grid didn't exist. I refused outright. I wouldn't be part of anything that isolated us from the context of the grid or turned us into a sideshow. Despite how they wanted to pitch it, there was a quiet respect between us. We rarely crossed paths, on or off the track, but I do remember one moment – meeting in the female toilets near the grid just before our race in Barcelona. She turned to me and I could see she was upset.

It's just so tough out there.

She was giving voice to emotions that I hadn't allowed to surface.

I know it is. But we have to keep pushing, I said, trying to offer a bit of support.

She was right, though. It was tough. Both of us were constantly fighting the perception that being beaten by a girl was somehow shameful. I even noticed it with one of my younger teammates who had graduated from F3. The team would come over the radio and tease him: *Ha, you got beaten by a girl.*

Comments like that didn't just make things harder for him, they made things harder for *me*. It reinforced the idea that I wasn't on the same level, that losing to me was something to be embarrassed about.

Not long after, I was unexpectedly assigned a grid boy instead of the traditional grid girl. Typically, grid slots were marked by women dressed in the sponsor's branding, but at my car, a man stood in their place, dressed in white from head to toe. It felt like another stunt – an unnecessary attempt to single me out again as 'the female driver'. Photographers swarmed, eager to capture this oddity. I was furious.

After the race, I approached the DTM organisers to express my frustration.

This is motorsport, I told them. *I don't care if it's a man or a woman marking my grid slot, but please stop treating me differently.*

When the grid boy appeared again at the next race, I went again to the organisers.

This has to stop.

It was the last time the grid boy made an appearance.

I was determined to fight every effort to make me into 'the female driver'. Motorsport had never been about being that for me – it was about the stopwatch, about proving myself against every driver on that grid. I wasn't going to let them reduce it to a battle of marketing gimmicks and me as a token, there for appearances only. I was there to race, on the same terms as everyone else.

But then came the next curveball. A call from Norbert.

Okay. Are you ready for some news? I've got good news and bad news. What do you want first?

I didn't even hesitate.

Bad news. Always better to get it over and done with.

He paused for a second, like he was bracing for my reaction.

Your car next year is going to be pink.

I groaned. *No, Norbert. You're joking.*

Silence.

If that's the bad news, what's the good news?

Well . . . he said, dragging it out. *We're going to put some white on it too.*

Not exactly the kind of good news I was hoping for. And in reality, the white was barely there. A token strip, almost an afterthought. The car was pink – proper pink. And to make it even worse, stamped right on the roof was the face of a blonde woman from a budget TV gossip magazine.

A blonde girl driving a pink car, covered in tabloid branding.

Could it get any more cliché?

I absolutely hated it.

But there was nothing I could do. It was the sponsor's choice. No arguments, no negotiations.

At first, every time I saw the car, I cringed. I didn't want to be that driver – the one people wouldn't take seriously, the stereotype. It wasn't about the colour itself, it was what it represented. Another gimmick. Another way to single me out when all I wanted was to be treated the same.

But then, something entirely unexpected happened.

At the races, I started seeing little girls, more than ever before, lining up, watching, completely captivated. Dressed head to toe in pink. Their fathers would come up to me and say, *She only wanted to come because of the pink car.*

Well, that stopped me in my tracks.

Many had the same question: *Is it the Hello Kitty car?*

At first, I laughed it off. Thought nothing of it. But to have girls talking to me about my car was completely new, and I was enjoying it. So I started telling them, *You know what? It is. But it's in disguise.*

Hello Kitty was huge at the time, and suddenly, after a few of these conversations, I realised: my car wasn't *just* a pink race car. It was a reason for these young girls to be there. A reason for them to look at motorsport differently.

It made me rethink everything.

I went from hating the idea of the pink car to realising something bigger: *representation matters*. Me being so visible in this bubblegum-coloured race car was making little girls excited about racing. It was as fast as the other cars on the track, but better than that, it brought the possibility of more girls following on after me. Maybe it wasn't so bad after all.

Even though I was fully embedded in the Mercedes team and clearer in my ambitions than ever, I always kept my guard up off the track. I had my own rules from the very beginning – I didn't date other drivers. I didn't want anyone on the track to think I was romantically involved with someone I was racing against, so I never let it happen. However, there was someone who always made an effort to come and speak to me: Thomas, the team manager of Audi. As he wasn't in my team, he understood what I was going through, but wasn't directly involved in my world. Our conversations had a different dynamic – one that felt separate from the pressures of racing. Of course, the fact that he was a team manager at Audi and I was driving for Mercedes made things complicated. We never talked about racing. It was an unspoken rule. He was simply a gentleman, and in a paddock where everything felt like a competition, that stood out. Funny, with an upbeat can-do attitude, he was well regarded, the kind of person no one had a bad word to say about.

As we got closer, I started visiting him in Germany and I got to know his family, who were warm and welcoming. They only spoke German, which meant that my language skills continued to improve, and I was always invited to join them for mealtimes. Living alone in Switzerland had been isolating, but Thomas was only a two-hour drive away.

We enjoyed spending time together, and he always treated me with such respect. We never argued – there was a comfort in how our lives fitted together. He was wonderful with my family too. When Mo, Grandma and Mum came to visit, he met them at the airport with flowers and went out of his way to make them feel welcome.

But my personal life was still separate from my racing life, and it stayed that way. I was always aware that perception mattered in the paddock. He couldn't come to any Mercedes events with me, that went without saying, but over time, it became an issue for me. In a profession as all-consuming as motorsport, I realised I couldn't keep the personal separate from the professional: there weren't enough hours in the day. I could never fully let my guard down. I was on my own for the majority of the time, and ultimately, I still felt alone.

Back home in Scotland after my season had finished, we were all gathered in the kitchen. My mum was speaking warmly about Thomas – how kind he was, how grateful she was that I had someone like him in my life. I stood there, listening, saying nothing. When she left the room to fetch something, Mo turned to me quietly and said, *You're not sure about Thomas, are you?*

I hesitated. How could I explain a feeling I barely understood myself? He was so good to me. On paper, there was nothing wrong – nothing not to like. But beneath the surface, something didn't sit right. A quiet unease I had pushed down.

I was never going to be a German housewife. He'd mentioned it in passing – soft suggestions about when I would stop racing: building a house, settling down, having children. Over time, I realised that wasn't the life I wanted.

I just don't see myself living the life he's imagined for us, I said.

I wasn't ready to step away from the track. I craved challenge, not comfort.

Then you need to end it, Susie.

It will be really difficult, Mo.

If it's not right, you need to get out.

When I got back, the conversation with Mo circling in my mind, I tried to bring it up – my feeling that something wasn't right, that I wasn't happy. But he brushed it off. He was so certain of us, so sure we were happy, that my doubts never seemed to register. After a few tries, I gave up. Mo had been right: if I didn't leave, we would trundle along and then leaving would seem impossible. So, I packed my bags. And I think that was the first time it really hit either of us – that it was really over. I got on with things, as I always had, but this sense of solitude, something I was used to by now, was beginning to feel different. I was very much on my own again.

An event where this came into sharp focus was the Hugo Boss Christmas party. It was being held near Metzingen, the same place I'd visited earlier that year, and it was a big event, celebrating the achievements of Hugo Boss's sponsored athletes that season. I found myself seated at the top table, along with some of the most powerful and influential figures in F1, including Norbert and Lewis Hamilton.

I wasn't intimidated. I wasn't nervous. By that point, I had established myself and the evening was great fun – athletes like Ukrainian heavyweight boxers the Klitschko brothers were there, cracking jokes on stage with Lewis.

As the night wore on, the conversation drifted towards an exclusive world – the glamour and excess of Formula One: yachts in St Tropez, private jets, endless parties. Was it showing off? Or was I simply too detached from that kind of life? Either way, I wasn't envious – it was entertaining to listen to.

The evening had been good fun. Everyone was in high spirits, and as we piled into the shuttles back to the hotel, it was clear where the night was headed. The bar. But for me, there was never a question as I didn't drink. I went straight to my room. Not for a second did I consider joining them. I never did.

I got into bed and fell into a deep sleep. The phone in the room rang. I blinked, still half-asleep, and looked at the clock – it was after 2 a.m. I tried to register what was happening. The hotel phone? At this time? That never happened. I picked it up. A voice – low, male, slurred – murmuring something about the bar, the night still going. And then I recognised it.

My brain scrambled. I let out a half-laugh, polite but confused. *Yeah, yeah*, I murmured, trying to match his tone, waiting for the conversation to end. But something about it was off. He was drunk, clearly. And then, before he could say anything more, I put the phone down. Awkward – he was one of the most powerful men in F1 and could have had the ability to make or break my career.

A beat of silence. Then the phone rang again.

I exhaled sharply.

This time, his voice was lower, more direct.

What's your room number? I'm coming to your room.

I forced a laugh, light, dismissive. *No, no, don't come to my room.* I put the phone down again.

A pause.

Then it rang again.

That was it. I yanked the cord from the wall, my heart now thudding in my chest. Awkward had shifted to uneasy. My mind rationalised it – just drunk, just having fun. He would call it a day soon enough. I lay back down.

And then the knocking on my door.

I shot up, my heart hammering.

A voice outside the door. The door handle started moving.

A split second of frozen panic. *Think, Susie, think. Stay calm.* I moved quickly, wedging the desk chair under the door handle. I sat on the edge of the bed, my eyes fixed on the handle. It jerked again. *What am I going to do if that door opens?* I couldn't think of anyone I could call to help me.

Stay calm, Susie.

I mapped the room. The wardrobe. The door to the stairwell. If he managed to force his way in, I'd slip into the wardrobe, wait, and the second I had an opening, I'd run. I knew where the stairs were. I could be in reception in seconds.

I was shaking, terrified. Forcing myself to take deep breaths. *Stay calm. Stay in control.*

The thudding stopped. Silence.

I didn't move. The adrenaline coursed through me. I slowly lay down, staring at the ceiling. There was no chance of sleep. By three in the morning, I had one thought: when's the earliest I can leave? I didn't want to see anyone at breakfast.

By 5.30, I was packed, out the door and in my car, already heading back to Switzerland. I didn't stop. I didn't look back. I was on edge, and it took me a few days to sleep properly again. Then the doubt crept in. Was it really such a big deal? Was I overreacting?

All I knew was that it left a knot in my stomach, a lingering unease. Saying nothing to anyone, not even my parents, felt easier. Compartmentalise. Move on.

January came, and with it, new plans. I was told I'd be heading to the Australian F1 Grand Prix in March. My first time in Australia. On the Friday ahead of the race weekend I would be hosting an AMG Ladies' Day, the guests being a select group of customers and leading female personalities from the region. A new concept. I had a Hugo Boss shift dress picked out, beige, sleeveless and belted.

I arrived at the event to find the McLaren-Mercedes lounge completely transformed – AMG branding, elegant floral arrangements, champagne, and a crowd of stylishly dressed women, many experiencing a Formula One race for the first time. Overlooking the track, the lounge had a lively yet relaxed atmosphere. We watched the practice sessions, enjoyed lunch and let the conversation flow effortlessly.

Then, an announcement. We were able to go and visit the Formula One paddock. I smiled and nodded. But inside, I felt it. A sharp twist of unease.

I glanced down at my dress. The beige shift. The belt. The high heels.

I should've brought a change of clothes.

The paddock wasn't just any place. It was my working environment. And in that moment, I didn't want to be there like this. Not in a dress. As we arrived, that feeling settled deeper in my gut. Walking in, I felt completely out of place.

I wasn't part of Ladies' Day anymore.

I was a Mercedes driver.

And I should've been in my team kit, not a dress and heels.

We were taken to visit the garage, then brought to the McLaren F1 hospitality area. I walked in, barely a minute inside, when suddenly – there he was. The man who had tried to enter my room.

I hadn't seen him approach. Hadn't noticed him in the room. He just appeared.

He looked at me. Held out his hand.

I owe you an apology.

That was it.

I shook his hand. I know I'm not the only one who's ever found themselves in that position. It's familiar territory – the quiet calculation you have to make in the aftermath. Was this a one-off? A moment of bad judgement? Or is this someone who crosses lines because they feel entitled to? That kind of judgement call weighs heavily, especially when it lands squarely on you.

I didn't believe this man was a predator. He had made a mistake, recognised it and apologised. But that doesn't erase the fact that the night had left me shaken. And that's the part that's so particular to the female experience – how quickly the room can shift, how fast we're made to question our safety, our instincts, our own role in the moment. And at the time, the idea of telling someone didn't even feel like an option. It wasn't how the world worked back then.

Although things have changed, it's still an uphill struggle, especially when power and influence are involved. There are still men who would rather silence than be held accountable, and for women, the cost of speaking out remains far too high.

11

Bᴀᴄᴋ from Australia, I was emailing with my engineer about preparing for the first race weekend when a Facebook notification pinged on my laptop. A friend request had come in from someone I didn't know. I was about to disregard it until a message appeared.

You don't know me but I'm a friend of Toto Wolff.

He had my attention. I accepted the friend request and then another message arrived.

I'm sitting with Toto right now, we're in Miami and I've persuaded him to join Facebook.

Then a Facebook request arrived from Toto, with a message: *I'm new to all of this, am not entirely convinced.*

I looked at his page. His status was single. *I think your page looks good,* I replied, *but you need to get all your details right. It says you're single.*

I am single now.

I stopped in my tracks. Miss Austria was gone. I raised an eyebrow.

At races, I'd seen Toto around, but we had never connected, never said more than a few polite words to each other. In my head, he was with Miss Austria and very much off my radar. I had found out he had raced successfully himself and was now managing young drivers, one of them being a teammate of mine. He had also invested in HWA, the company building and running the DTM cars for Mercedes-Benz Motorsport, but I knew nothing of the details.

A week later, I flew to a three-day pre-season test. It was during one of the lunch breaks that Hans-Jürgen Mattheis, the team manager, walked in. His expression gave nothing away at first, but then he informed us that Toto Wolff had been in a serious accident while trying to break the lap record at the Nürburgring. Only afterwards did I realise how narrowly he'd escaped. The car had hit the barrier at over 290kph, spun through 180 degrees, and ricocheted across the track, slamming into steel guardrails with such force that the impact tore nearly every bolt from the seat.

My heart raced. Hans-Jürgen turned to Gary Paffett, the de facto team leader, and suggested one of the drivers should call Toto to wish him a speedy recovery. Gary barely missed a beat before glancing at me.

Yeah, good idea. Susie, you do it.

Hans-Jürgen nodded.

Okay, Susie, I'll send you his contact details.

And just like that, I had his number and a reason to call.

When I got back from the test, I made sure to find the right moment and thought through my opening words. I took a breath and dialled his number.

Hi, Toto. It's Susie Stoddart. We heard about your crash and wanted to wish you a speedy recovery. We're all thinking of you . . .

There was the briefest pause before he answered.

That's so nice of you to call.

He asked me about the DTM car, how it was to drive, my thoughts on the upcoming season. He told me about the record attempt – how the tyre blew, how he'd lost his sense of smell, how bad his back was. We laughed. It felt natural, effortless and I didn't want the call to end. Before we knew it an hour had passed and he realised he was late for a meeting.

I've got to go. But I'm coming to the presentation in Düsseldorf next week. I'll see you there. And just like that, Düsseldorf took on a whole new meaning.

I couldn't wait to get there.

The night before the presentation in Düsseldorf, a team dinner was scheduled. I spent the week planning my outfit and was looking forward to seeing Toto. I realised this was a kind of nerves I'd never felt before – forget fight or flight, these were fluttering butterflies that no amount of compartmentalisation could control. I couldn't stop thinking about him. The anticipation grew until, at last, it was time to go to the restaurant.

I arrived, trying to appear composed, but inside, my heart was pounding. I scanned the room but couldn't see him. At first, I thought perhaps something had come up, maybe a delayed flight or a last-minute work issue. I kept stealing glances at the door, willing him to walk in. But he never did. By the time I returned to the hotel, the anticipation had drained from me, I felt deflated and disappointed. What a letdown.

The following morning, I was despondent and knew there was a high chance he would not show up at all. I figured I'd just head down to breakfast in my race suit; there was no need to make too much of an effort this time. Then, there he was, sitting at one of the tables, smiling and chatting. My face lit up before I could stop it, and just like that, the butterflies came back.

I joined his table, and he asked how the dinner was. I, in turn, asked why he hadn't come. His reply? He had called to ask where it was, only to be told by one of my teammates not to bother coming – it was pretty boring. What? I was there!

After looking forward to seeing him, after wondering all evening if he'd turn up, it turned out he had been in town all along. So frustrating. But as we talked, my mood lightened. Like our telephone conversation, it was easy and natural. Before I knew it, it was time to go. The rest of my day was packed full; I was busy driving the car in a show run, but I still found myself trying to spot Toto at every opportunity.

During the lunch break, we ended up in a large group, and the conversation shifted to everyone's love lives. I stayed silent, hoping to avoid any questions, until our team manager said, *Susie, don't you think it's time you tried to finally date someone from Mercedes?*

I forced a laugh, avoiding Toto's eyes, willing my face not to betray anything.

Well, there's nobody from Mercedes, I said lightly.

And then, Toto looked at me, putting both hands in the air, and exclaimed with a smile, *What about me?*

Everyone laughed. My face went scorching hot. I felt it, I knew it, and there was nothing I could do about it. I didn't even dare look up, just a half-laugh. The conversation moved on, but my thoughts stayed right there. Occasionally, we would glance at each other. Was he serious? Was it a joke? I couldn't tell.

The rest of the afternoon passed in a hectic blur. When the presentation was finished, I headed back to the hotel, hoping to see him. But he was nowhere to be seen. I got into my car for the long drive back to Switzerland, and after about twenty minutes, I realised I couldn't just leave things as they were. I didn't want to live with the regret of never telling him how I truly felt. I pulled into a fuel station, my heart pounding. I typed out a text, then deleted it. Typed it again. Deleted it again. Finally, I settled on something simple:

Toto, I just wanted to let you know – if it had to be someone from Mercedes, it would only ever be you. Susie.

Terrifying. I had never put myself out there like this. I sat there, staring at the message. My finger hovered over the send button. What if he didn't feel the same? What if I made things awkward? But then, before I could talk myself out of it, I pressed send, squeezed my eyes shut and threw my phone onto the passenger seat. I turned up the music and got back onto the motorway, trying to pretend I hadn't just put my heart on the line.

Minutes later, my phone buzzed. His name flashed on the screen. My pulse shot through the roof. I pulled into the next lay-by, took a deep breath, and opened the message.

That's really nice to hear, Susie. I'm just about to jump on a plane, but I'll call you as soon as I land.

Not overly enthusiastic, no, but not dismissive either. The drive home felt like an eternity. Every time my phone lit up, my stomach flipped. When I finally got home, the call came through.

Well that text was unexpected.

I laughed. *In a good or bad way?*

Good . . . Definitely good . . .

We stayed on the phone for three hours and from that point on talked to each other daily. We knew we would see each other again at the next race weekend. Even before we saw each other again, it felt right.

On one of those early calls he said something that would set the tone for our whole relationship: *Listen, let's not play any games. I will always be honest and direct with you in how I'm feeling and what I'm thinking.*

For the first time, my defences were being challenged – the armour I had always relied on was met with someone insisting on honesty and openness, matching it with their own. His empathy meant I felt a newfound willingness to let someone in, to be unguarded, authentic and truly honest. I found myself sharing not just my thoughts but my insecurities as well. I started talking to him about the struggles I'd been facing in racing – the pink car, the constant battle to be taken seriously, the frustration of knowing I was capable of more but not having the results to back it up. I should have been fighting further up the grid, but I didn't have the latest car. It all poured out, and he listened. Really listened. His responses were straightforward, no fluff:

Who cares about the pink car? The only thing that matters is the performance. And who cares if you wear a dress or a trouser suit? Wear what feels right to you – be authentic. Above all, just be you.

I'd always prided myself on staying true to who I was, but hearing it from him reinforced it. He reminded me that people would always have opinions, some in my favour, some against me, but none of it mattered. I just had to keep going my way, blocking out the noise. And that was the thing about Toto – he wasn't telling me anything I didn't already know, but he made me feel it. Made me believe it more than ever.

Following on from the race weekend, we agreed that I'd visit him in Vienna as he was heading there to see his family. I had my own assumptions about what his place would be like: full of computers, given he worked in finance. I pictured a mess – definitely a bachelor pad.

As it turned out, my pressing concern in the lead-up to that trip was less about his living situation and more about my own face. Whether it was the anticipation or something else entirely, I had developed a massive spot on my chin just before I flew out. The kind that no amount of concealer could hide.

When I landed in Vienna and came out of arrivals, I didn't see him anywhere. I sent him a quick message: *I've landed.*

His response? *Sorry, I'm on my way.*

That was my introduction to the fact that Toto Wolff runs late. Always. Eventually, he arrived, and I noticed right away that he couldn't stop glancing at my chin. I tried to ignore it, but after a while, I had to laugh.

Listen, you can say it, I told him. *I know I have a huge spot on my chin.*

He let out a breath of relief. *Thank goodness you said something. That's a really big spot.*

We both laughed. We've never stopped making each other laugh since.

When we got to his house, I suddenly realised just how far off my expectations had been. The moment I stepped inside, it was clear that I couldn't have been more wrong about the bachelor pad.

Toto had an incredible eye for detail. His place wasn't just tidy; it was immaculate. Every piece of furniture, every work of art, every design choice was considered and curated. It wasn't just about keeping things neat – it was about creating something beautiful. He took me to his favourite restaurants, places he'd known forever, where the waiters greeted him like an old friend. We walked hand in hand along the grand old streets lined with imperial facades. It was romance on another level.

I could have burst with happiness. That magnetic pull I had felt the first time I saw him had only grown stronger, deepening with every moment we spent together. These days in Vienna had revealed more of him, and with each passing hour,

I *knew*. By the end of the weekend, the words had been said. We were in love.

We spent every moment we could together. He lived nearby in Switzerland, making it easy. During the week, I'd drive to his apartment. One evening, about thirty minutes into a movie, he suddenly paused it. I assumed he needed the bathroom, but instead, he walked out and returned with a ladder.

Without a word, he climbed up and adjusted a spotlight on the ceiling by maybe two centimetres.

I watched, half amused, half baffled. He stepped back, tilted his head, then bent down for another look before finally nodding.

That's so much better, he said.

The attention to detail, the precision, the need for things to be exactly right. I had found my match.

One evening on my way back home from a test, he called.

I have to go to Mallorca this weekend. Can you join me? I'll pick you up in Altenrhein.

I paused. *Altenrhein? Why are you picking me up in Altenrhein?*

There's a small private airport there, he said. It was a very 'Thomas Crown' moment, seeing him land, casually stepping out to greet me and continuing our journey to Mallorca as if it were the most normal thing in the world.

He had some business to take care of – visiting Hans Werner Aufrecht at his home there as they were joint shareholders in HWA. When he returned, we decided to go for a swim. We were messing around in the sea when he casually said, *I'll race you back to the beach.*

I didn't think much of it. *All right*, I said.

The moment he took off, I went for it. Within seconds, I realised he had underestimated me. He lifted his head to check his position, and by the time he looked back, I was already ahead. I reached the beach first and turned to see him arrive a few seconds later, looking shocked. Once again, my swimming skills had the power to surprise.

I didn't know you could swim like that, he said, still catching his breath.

I used to race when I was younger.

Right. Impressive.

Later, when we were lying on the beach, he disappeared a couple of times. I figured he was taking work calls, as he often did, so I didn't think much of it.

Then, on our last day, he suggested another swim.

I laughed. *You really want to do this after I completely destroyed you last time?*

He just smiled.

We started the race, and immediately, something was different. He was faster. A lot faster. Suddenly, I had to give everything just to keep up. We were neck and neck, both pushing, both refusing to give in, but he edged past me, reaching the beach first.

We lay on the sand, laughing. *Well, you've definitely improved*, I said.

Yeah, I watched some swimming tutorials on YouTube to figure out how to improve my stroke and practised in the pool.

It was classic Toto – competitive in everything, unwilling to accept defeat, even in something as trivial as a swimming race. But more than that, it was funny, and it was *us*.

After a few months, Toto wanted me to meet his children, Benedict and Rosi. Still young at the time, they lived in Vienna with their mother, Stephanie, his ex-wife. Though they had divorced when the children were little, Toto remained a constant presence in their lives. Both Toto and Stephanie were committed to putting the children first. They never raised their voices in front of them or allowed tensions to spill over. I respect her fully for welcoming me into their lives and never making things difficult.

It became a natural step for me to join Toto and the kids at the weekend. But natural doesn't always mean easy. I'd spent so long as a fiercely independent racing driver, used to life on the road, solo routines, full focus. Suddenly, there were two young children, aged five and eight, looking up at me. I wasn't their mother and I had to figure out where I sat in this new dynamic. It was new territory, uncharted, and I didn't want to overstep but in turn wanted both children to feel they had someone they could always turn to for support without ever feeling I was judging or intruding.

It took time. Stepping into someone else's family story is never simple, especially when children are involved and there's history that pre-dates you. But everyone made an effort, I was invited to join Christmas and birthday celebrations and I realised slowly that I didn't need to feel under any pressure, I didn't need to replace anyone, they already had a great mother. What I could be was someone they could always count on. Someone solid. Someone who showed up. And that realisation took me back to my own childhood – how much my parents gave me, how steady they were in the background. I wanted to bring that same sense of security.

It was a balancing act. One we all had to navigate together. And it wasn't perfect, it never is, but what held all of us steady was mutual respect. For the past, for each other, and most importantly, for the kids. I didn't try to be their mother. I bit my tongue at certain moments, holding back and rather waiting for my opinion to be asked, and if it wasn't, I didn't interfere. But I did everything I could to give them a foundation of love and trust. That part came naturally because they were wonderful kids.

Six months later, Toto had a board meeting just outside Venice, and since I'd never been before, we agreed to meet there for the weekend. When I arrived at the hotel, he was already in the room. He'd just dropped his bags and rushed out earlier for his meeting – clothes draped over furniture, shoes kicked off in a hurry. I went to hang up his jacket and trousers.

No, no, no, don't touch anything, he said.

I stopped, a little confused. *I'm just hanging your clothes up.*

Yeah, just . . . leave my stuff alone, please.

I thought that was strange: he was usually so meticulous, but I let it go.

We spent the day walking through Venice, taking in the winding streets, bustling piazzas and quiet canals. We rode a gondola and wandered through galleries, soaking up the art and atmosphere. Venice was beautiful, timeless, full of life. It was romantic but I could sense something in him – an edge, a slight nervousness that didn't quite fit. A couple of times, he stepped away to take phone calls, which I assumed were work-related, though they seemed to pull his focus in a way that even business calls normally didn't.

That evening, he took me to Harry's Bar, Venice's most iconic restaurant. But the moment we stepped inside, he glanced across the room and tensed.

I know that family over there, he said, nodding towards a table a few rows away.

Oh, okay, I replied, expecting him to brush it off.

They're from Austria. I know them.

That was it. But the way he said it, the fact that it seemed to bother him, struck me as odd. Why would it matter? The next day, we continued exploring Venice, but again, he disappeared for phone calls. I noticed it, but I didn't push. It wasn't completely out of character for him, after all. Later, we packed up and took a taxi boat to the airport. As we floated along, I turned to him.

That was such a nice trip, I said.

He hesitated for a moment, then replied, *Well, we haven't actually left Venice yet.*

I laughed. *Yes, we have.*

No, we haven't.

We have. We're literally on our way to the airport.

Then, without another word, he reached into his pocket and pulled out a beautiful diamond solitaire ring.

For a moment, I just stared at it. The city stretched out on one side, the airport ferry terminal on the other, and then came the realisation of what was happening.

But Toto, you have to ask the question, I finally said, breaking the silence.

He blinked. *Okay, okay – will you marry me?*

I didn't even let him finish before I was saying, *Yes, yes, yes, yes, yes.*

When we arrived at the airport, I called my parents to share the news – we were engaged. I was on cloud nine. Only later would I learn that he had bought the ring just six weeks after we started seeing each other.

We initially thought it would be nice to get married in Scotland. Mo was ill with cancer by that time, and I really wanted her to be there with me, so we settled on the idea of a small wedding in a Scottish castle. We visited three, trying to find the perfect place. Then, heartbreakingly, Mo passed away. Like with all my grandparents, she and I were incredibly close. She was my confidante, someone I looked up to and turned to when life became difficult. Without her, the idea of a wedding in Scotland no longer felt right – it felt hollow. And so, we turned our thoughts to Austria instead.

We couldn't decide between the mountains or Vienna, going back and forth without a clear answer. Then, in one of those conversations, a new idea emerged – why not choose somewhere that meant both sides of our family had to travel? A neutral, beautiful place where Scots and Austrians could come together. We settled on Capri. It was perfect. We loved Italy – its warmth, its way of life, its emphasis on family, laughter and effortless style. We visited a few times to finalise the details, choosing where we'd stay and how everything would unfold.

In London, Mum and I set out on a two-day search for a wedding dress. I'd done my research and knew exactly what I wanted – simple yet elegant. The first dress I tried on, we loved. Still, we kept looking, just to be sure. By the next morning, there was no doubt. I'd never been one to dream about my wedding or picture the perfect dress, but seeing myself in the mirror, I suddenly couldn't wait for the day to arrive.

We had planned a three-day celebration, keeping the guest list to just a hundred to ensure an intimate atmosphere. Narrowing it down was no easy task, but we followed a simple rule: we only wanted people we truly felt close to and who would genuinely enjoy celebrating with us.

The first day was for the formalities – the legal marriage, the paperwork – followed by a gathering to bring the Scots and Austrians together. The second day was the wedding itself, and the third, a relaxed brunch to round it all off.

My oldest school friend from Oban, Heidi, stood by my side as a bridesmaid, along with Rosi. Benedict was our ring bearer. Both of us being detail-oriented, we brought in wedding planners, who certainly had their work cut out with us. Among them was Julia Pahle, an Austrian whose efficiency stood out so much that we later invited her to join our team, and who is still with us today.

On the first morning, we woke up knowing that, as the tradition has it, we wouldn't be staying together that night. But something was off. Toto was unusually quiet.

I looked at him. *Is everything okay?*

He nodded. *It's fine.*

I wasn't convinced. *Are you sure?*

He hesitated before saying, *Well, I made a list.*

A list?

Of positives and negatives.

I blinked. *Of what?*

Of getting married. Of getting married to you, he said. *There are definitely more positives than negatives.*

I stared at him for a second, shaking my head in disbelief. I normally appreciated his honesty and directness but making a list, on the day of our wedding?

Toto, I don't care what's on that list. We are getting married today.

I never did find out what was on that list, and now, fifteen years later, Toto assures me he was just joking.

We got married that day, and then had our church ceremony the next. We had searched Capri for the perfect little church and my local minister from Oban was there to officiate. A bagpiper from the local pipe band flew in, giving a Scottish touch to the proceedings.

Afterwards, hand in hand, we led a procession through the town with our guests following. Locals and tourists stopped to watch, smiling, clapping, some even cheering. By the middle of the dinner, guests were already on the tables dancing – it turns out the Scots had bet the Austrians they could handle their drink better. So we abandoned the dessert and cake, moving straight into party mode, which lasted nearly all night.

Leading up to the wedding, a point of contention became my surname. After the wedding, I would have one race left that season and I made it known that I would need the name on my car changed. The Mercedes marketing department pulled me aside: my entire career with them had been built on my surname – Stoddart was what people recognised – and they strongly advised me to keep it in racing for continuity.

I didn't hesitate. *Absolutely not.* When I told Toto, he shrugged.

Do whatever feels right. I'll be proud if you become a Wolff, but I'll understand if you stay Stoddart.

But for me, there was never a question. I was becoming a Wolff.

For the first time, I wasn't just fighting for myself. I wasn't on my own anymore. I was part of a team. And I wanted everyone to know that. I had designed a helmet for the last race with my new surname and Toto's helmet design on one side with my own on the other. When I arrived at the track, the team had put a big sticker on the back of my race car – 'Just Married' – which I asked them to leave on for the race.

12

MARRIED life didn't slow us down. By the end of our first year together, Toto had invested in a minority stake in the Williams F1 team, so alongside DTM, we began travelling to selected F1 races. I thrived on the constant movement – new countries, new cultures, always on the road. Home life was reduced to a few days a week, just long enough to unpack, repack and head off again. The only real constant was our weekends with the children – our anchor in an otherwise whirlwind existence.

Saturday morning tennis became my joint programme with the kids. Since my tennis skills left much to be desired, we limited David, the coach, to a few quick drills before launching into our main event: doubles. Me and Benedict versus Rosi and David.

These matches grew increasingly competitive. Benedict and I realised our best shot at winning was to hit every ball to Rosi, forcing her to dash around the court while David stayed mostly out of play. Poor Rosi – by the end, she was exhausted, and at least one of the kids was guaranteed to storm off in a huff. We'd walk home with rackets in hand and emotions running high, while Toto, baffled by the drama, would ask how a simple tennis lesson could cause so much upset. But the tension never lingered, and I loved the time we spent together. Between weekends and family holidays, we built a bond of our own. We've since graduated to padel, and now it's boys versus girls.

Although our schedules often pulled us in different directions, we always made the effort to be no more than a week apart. One trip took me to California, where AMG had taken over the legendary Laguna Seca circuit to launch their new GT car. I spent three days at the track, giving hot laps to clients, pushing the car to its limits. Toto had managed to align a US work trip with the event and planned to join me on the last day. By then, I had every inch of the circuit memorised – I was drifting through corners, completely at ease in the car.

When he arrived that afternoon, I was eager to take him out for a lap. Toto has never been a great passenger, so I knew I had to be perfect. I wheel-spun out of the pit lane and attacked the first two corners. Over the engine noise, I heard him, faint but firm:

Whoa, whoa, whoa, whoa.

I ignored him. He's a racer, after all. I kept my foot planted, hitting the throttle early to drift through the exits. By the time I hit the end of the main straight, we reached nearly 280kph. On the exit of the third corner, he was shouting.

I've had enough. Stop the car.

I pulled over. *What's wrong?*

He didn't answer. The passenger door flew open and he was already walking away. When I returned to the pits he said, *Too much, Susie. You might have spent three days around this track, but I've just come off a long flight.*

I didn't think of it again, but Toto obviously decided he was going to get his own back. He loved rallying and in 2006 was the vice Austrian Rally Champion. Some months later, he planned a test day out in the winding forest tracks in Austria with his rally friends and invited me to come along. I had never sat in a rally car before so had no clue what to expect. I started in the passenger seat while Toto drove, and I was blown away by the sheer speed of it, how precise you had to be, how little room there was for error. If you made a mistake, you weren't just running wide onto a bit of tarmac – you were off into the trees. No runoff areas, no smooth kerbs – just raw, unforgiving terrain. It was exhilarating. And I have to say, I was definitely a better passenger than Toto.

Then it was my turn to get behind the wheel – Toto in the passenger seat, shouting advice, pushing me far beyond my comfort zone in a bid to make me respectable on the timing screen. By the end of each session, we'd be covered in dust, exhausted but high with adrenaline. It took time to recalibrate my instincts, to grasp how radically different the technique was – how early you had to set up for corners, how much faith you had to place in the car, and how commitment was every-thing. That was the start of us rallying together and every year we now have a family tradition of going ice rallying after Christmas.

On one particular test, I kept bleeding time through a fast, sweeping right-hander – my minimum speed was too low compared to Toto's. I decided it was time to fully commit. The runoff led into a field, so I had some margin for error.

On my next attempt, I kept my foot flat, lifting only for the briefest moment. It felt good – until the corner tightened more than I'd anticipated. I wasn't going to make it. The rear snapped, and suddenly, I was off.

Before I knew it, I was flying sideways – not just into any field but straight into a cornfield. The car bounced violently as stalks of corn slammed into the windscreen like a barrage of rocks. The impact cracked the glass in multiple places until I could barely see.

I limped the car back to the trucks, where everyone immediately turned to stare.

What happened to you? Toto asked.

I got corn on the cobbed.

And that was it. From that moment on, it became a running joke – Susie fancied some sweetcorn for dinner, so she decided to collect a few cobs on her way.

We also both loved karting, just the two of us, head-to-head – pure, unfiltered racing. Testing at different tracks for fun, we relished every battle, trading positions and pushing each other to the limit. But no matter what Toto tried – tweaking setups, ordering special soft qualifying tyres, putting extra weight on my kart – he could never beat my lap time. Karting was my hunting ground.

*   *   *

It was during those days, out there pushing myself in the rally car and karting, that I was reminded just how much I loved racing. It only amplified what I already knew – I was no longer happy in DTM.

I had been stuck in the midfield for too long. I had never made it into the factory team with a new car. And to be fair, I didn't have the results to argue that I deserved it either. But that didn't change the feeling that I was stagnant, that I wasn't progressing anymore.

I had grown comfortable. I was earning great money, representing Mercedes-Benz on a global stage, surrounded by a team with whom I had built strong friendships. Everything about my situation was safe and stable. But deep down, the frustration over my lack of results was gnawing at me, growing louder with every race weekend.

At first, I tried to suppress it. I told myself to be grateful. After all, I had an incredible opportunity. I was in a position many would dream of. But it got to a point where I couldn't ignore it anymore. My gut was screaming at me: this isn't enough. I needed more. I needed to keep moving forward.

I told Toto that I was seriously considering leaving DTM. His response was direct, as always: *Okay, well, what are you going to do next?*

I looked at him and said, *I don't know yet. But I just know it's not this.*

That gut instinct had guided me through so many moments in my career, and I knew I had to trust it again.

So towards the end of that season, I called Norbert Haug. It was one of the hardest conversations I'd ever had. I told him that the following year would be my last in DTM. He was immediately taken aback – he just couldn't comprehend why I was stopping.

I tried to explain. I had never given less than everything in DTM, but I had also not met my own expectations. I had reached my ceiling there. And as a racing driver, I needed more than just showing up. I needed results, I needed progress, I needed that sense of achievement to justify all the work, all the sacrifices. Without it, I was starting to lose faith in myself. Maybe I'm not good enough. Maybe I was never fast enough.

DTM had only reinforced those doubts. Too often, I was left out on the worst strategy – not to fight for myself but to hold up the competition and protect a Mercedes win. I was a tool, a blocker, keeping the real contenders behind me. And every time I found myself in that role, it stung. I wanted to be the one chasing the wins, not the one slowing down the drivers who were.

Norbert tried to talk me out of it. He told me to take my time, to think it over, to not rush a decision. But I was firm: *No, this will be my last season.*

After that call, I sat down and wrote a formal letter to Mercedes. I thanked them for everything – for the opportunities, the experience, the years of support. But I made it clear: this was the end of my DTM chapter. It was time to move on.

The hardest part wasn't making the decision – it was what came after.

Everyone kept asking, *So, what are you doing next?*

And the truth was, I didn't know. I was twenty-nine – hardly retirement age. But I had always believed that sometimes, you have to close one door before another one can open. That belief gave me complete clarity. I never doubted my decision, never questioned myself. I knew it was the right thing for me.

At the same time, without realising it, I was starting to absorb more from Toto's world. His business world.

Every morning, he read the *Financial Times*, and he would hand me the occasional article he thought I might find interesting. Then, slowly, I started reading the *FT* on my own. Suddenly, I wanted to know more about what was happening in the world – beyond motorsport, beyond my bubble. It was the first time I had ever really paid attention to business, to global markets, to the way everything was interconnected. He was incredibly well informed, and I wanted to match that when I was at the table.

Toto always made a point of including me, even in meetings that had nothing to do with my world. He had already increased his stake in the Williams Formula One team and together with his childhood friend and business partner, Dr René Berger, the investment firm continued to invest in venture capital and the public markets. He'd invite me along to meetings with a simple offer:

Just listen. And if it's boring, you don't have to come next time.

But it was never boring.

* * *

I found myself engrossed by the discussions. There were nights when I hardly said a word, just taking it all in. In those rooms, there were often big egos, and in those environments, women at the table were hardly ever included in the discussion. But Toto would always make a point of turning to me and asking, *Susie, what do you think?*

Sometimes, I'd admit I didn't know enough about the subject to give an informed answer. But other times, I had a clear perspective. I understood racing, I understood teams, and it was a world I knew – at least from a sporting side, if not yet from a business perspective.

That was the shift. My perspective was widening, and for the first time, I was seeing the bigger picture. I was seeing beyond racing, beyond what happened on track. And that, in itself, was something Toto and I came to share – a curiosity about the wider world, an understanding that there was always more to learn.

Over time, Toto became increasingly involved with Williams. Coming from a private equity background, he typically avoided executive roles in the companies he invested in – but Williams was different. His passion for motorsport, coupled with his fiercely competitive nature, pulled him in. When the team's CEO, Adam Parr, resigned after the season opener in Melbourne, Bernie Ecclestone suggested that Toto step in, leading the team alongside Frank Williams.

I had first met Frank at the British round of DTM at Brands Hatch. Two of his former drivers, David Coulthard and Ralf Schumacher, were also racing for Mercedes. He was intrigued by the fact that Toto was married to a racing driver – especially a Scottish one. For a man of his generation, it was an unusual dynamic, something he wasn't accustomed to seeing. Every time we met after that, he wanted to talk about my racing and Scotland. As it turned out, he had been sent to boarding school there and had hated every minute of it. I did my best to convince him that Scotland wasn't as bad as he remembered. We had great conversations, and at some point, I mentioned that I had decided to leave DTM.

So, what's next? he asked, the same question I had been asked over and over.

I gave him the same honest answer. *I don't know. I just know it's not this.*

I told him I had always dreamed of making it to Formula One, but I had no roadmap anymore. I needed to see what opportunities were out there, what doors might open. I still loved racing. That hadn't changed. But this particular journey was coming to an end.

Frank looked at me for a moment, then his expression shifted. A glint in his eye.

He left and reappeared with Adam Parr.

We'll give you twenty-five laps.

I hesitated. *What do you mean?*

We'll give you twenty-five laps in our Formula One car. At Silverstone.

The words hung in the air.

For a split second, I was silent. Processing. A Formula One car.

I had spent my entire life dreaming of this moment. I wasn't naïve – were Frank and Adam offering it to impress Toto? That was a strong possibility. But I also knew one thing: when an opportunity presents itself, when a door opens, you don't stop to question why. You grab it with both hands.

That opportunity, those twenty-five laps, meant that I was suddenly being integrated into the Williams Formula One team. If I was going to drive that car, I had a hell of a lot to learn, and I had to be ready. It was agreed that I would get my chance at the end of the season. In the meantime, I was announced as a development driver, tasked with extensive simulator work and aerodynamic tests to prepare. With Formula One's testing restrictions tightened since 2009, opportunities to drive the car were rare – making every chance to gather data all the more valuable.

When I arrived at Williams, I was welcomed immediately. There was something about the team – it had a real sense of family. That resonated with me deeply. Claire Williams was there, already carving her own path within the team. There weren't many women in Formula One at the time, but she was always supportive. She wanted me to have this opportunity, and I felt that from the start.

A few months later news came that María de Villota, a Spanish driver, had been doing a straight-line F1 test for Marussia. On her way back to the truck, she had crashed, suffering severe head injuries. Just over a year later, she would die from complications related to that accident. At the time, I didn't know María well. But the news hit hard. It reinforced something I already knew – this was a big deal. Driving a Formula One car wasn't just another step in my career. It wasn't something to be taken lightly. It had to be done right.

I had always been meticulous in my preparation, but that sharpened my focus even more. My work ethic, my attention to detail – everything went up a level. I needed to be ready, not just for myself but for everyone who had put their faith in me.

I had got to know María after her accident, and that made it all feel even more real. I remember walking into the simulator the day after the crash and there was a collective silence. We all just looked at each other, as if to say, we can never let that happen again.

In the simulator I truly started to understand just how complex a Formula One car was. The sheer number of switches and buttons. The level of precision required just to get the car out of the garage. It was overwhelming at first, but I was determined to put myself in the best possible position to succeed.

Williams was just as committed to making sure I was fully prepared. This wasn't about ticking a box, about putting me in the car for the sake of it. They wanted me to take this test seriously. They put in the time, the effort, the resources. This only reinforced what I knew: that I wanted to be fast, to prove to myself that the fierce young girl who had so much belief in her speed was still there.

It was actually during one of those long simulator days, pushing myself to prepare for this moment, that I ended up proving once and for all that I wasn't ever going to be a domestic goddess.

Williams had installed an upgrade on the simulator, and by mid-morning, something went wrong. At around 11 a.m., the screens went blank. No dramatic bang, just an eerie shutdown. I climbed out of the car, expecting it to be a quick fix, but after some time, it became clear that this was a bigger issue.

Dave, who ran the simulator, eventually turned to me and said, *Okay, listen, go home. We're going to need all afternoon to fix this. We'll pick it up again in the morning.*

I wasn't about to argue. That meant an unexpected free afternoon, and I thought, *Great. I can get some work done.* But then, in a rare burst of domestic enthusiasm, I decided I was going to be a 'proper wife' and make Toto a really nice dinner. At this point, we mostly muddled through when it came to meals. My issue with cooking had always been that I made everything too healthy, which usually meant it didn't taste good. And I had a terrible habit of running out of patience midway through, convinced that I could be doing something more productive with my time.

But on this day, I had time. So I went to the organic shop, bought all sorts of fresh ingredients, ready to transform them into some kind of culinary masterpiece. While I was prepping, Toto called.

Hey, all good?

Yes, I'm at home already, I said. *The simulator broke down, so I figured I'd come back and make us a really nice dinner.*

There was a pause. *You're making dinner?*

Yes.

Another pause. Then, *Okay . . . that's unusual.*

But I was determined. I decided to make a vegetable soup, followed by a tasty chicken dish. So I started peeling vegetables, and before long, I was already beginning to get irritated by how long it was taking.

Eventually, Toto arrived home. The table was set, the candles were lit, and he looked genuinely surprised.

Wow, he said, surveying the scene. *This is very nice.*

I hope you enjoy it, I said proudly, sitting down as he took his first spoonful of soup.

There was a pause. Then he looked surprised. *I didn't know you could make fish soup . . .*

I stared at him. *It's not fish soup. It's vegetable soup.*

Another spoonful. Another frown. *Mmm . . . I don't know, Susie. This doesn't taste like vegetable soup.*

Only I could make vegetable soup taste like fish soup.

On to the chicken – my chance at redemption. Unfortunately, it was dry. Painfully dry. He chewed with forced politeness, then set down his fork, reached for his water and took a long sip – more an act of survival than refreshment.

You know what? he said. *Don't worry about cooking. That's just not your thing. You focus on all the things you do really well.*

We both laughed, and that was that – a masterful move on his part, and an opportunity I had no intention of passing up. From that moment on, we either ate out or stuck to the simplest, most foolproof meals at home. Any lingering notion of me becoming a highly domesticated wife ended right then and there.

While I was throwing everything into preparing for my Formula One test, I still wanted to finish my DTM season on a high. The final round was at Hockenheim, and as it approached, I realised how much it meant to me.

Walking into the paddock for that last weekend was emotional. DTM had been such a huge chapter of my life – not just my career but my entire life. Saying goodbye to the people who had been part of my journey, the team I had fought with, laughed with, struggled with, was harder than I expected.

No matter how ready I was to move on, I knew one thing for certain: DTM had played such a pivotal part in my life and I would forever thank my lucky stars for those years.

As soon as the final DTM race weekend was over, my entire focus shifted to Silverstone and the upcoming Formula One test. This was it – the moment I had been building towards. I needed to prove something – not only to the team but to myself. I needed to remind myself what I was capable of.

And the test went well. Really well.

The role of development driver evolved and I was later promoted to test driver, which meant getting back out on track – in a rookie test alongside other young drivers, and in an actual FP1 session. I would be driving in Free Practice at the British Grand Prix and then again at the German Grand Prix, back at Hockenheim – a circuit full of personal history for me. It was where I had made my DTM debut, where I had fought some of my toughest battles. And now, I was coming back in a Formula One car.

Life during that period was intense. I was constantly travelling, barely ever in one place for long. But I loved it because Toto and I were in it together. My role at Williams meant I was flying to Grand Prix weekends, and he was travelling non-stop as well, putting all of his time and energy into bringing the team back to its glory days. We were living a nomadic existence, bouncing between races, simulator sessions and our home in Switzerland. We loved it. We thrived in that rhythm, constantly on the move, always chasing the next challenge. We were completely, overwhelmingly happy.

The Spanish Grand Prix marked Williams' long-awaited comeback. Pastor Maldonado stunned the paddock by taking pole position and converting it into a victory – Williams' first in eight years. The Ferrari of Fernando Alonso was on his tail for the whole race but couldn't find a way past, and Maldonado held firm, delivering a win that reignited the team's prestige.

That triumph led to an unexpected call. Dr Wolfgang Bernhard, a fellow Austrian and Mercedes board member whom we knew from DTM, asked Toto to meet for coffee. Over their discussion, the core issue became clear – Mercedes had won just one race in three years, and the board wanted answers.

Toto, never one to criticise without understanding, said he'd need to do his due diligence before drawing conclusions.

However, from the outside, he already saw a fundamental disconnect. Mercedes Motorsport HQ in Stuttgart was worlds apart from the F1 team in Brackley. There had been a misguided assumption that buying the title-winning Brawn GP team would yield instant success. More critically, the board had been led to believe there would be a binding Resource Restriction Agreement, which limits spending, between teams. In reality, it was little more than a gentleman's agreement – problematic in a sport where few could truly be called gentlemen. Other teams had long disregarded the supposed spending cap, while Mercedes remained constrained by a self-imposed budget. The board had never been given a clear picture of the financial reality or its consequences.

After the meeting, Toto recounted the conversation to me. He had been as direct as ever.

Well, what are your expectations at Mercedes? he had asked them.

We want to win a World Championship, they replied.

Toto, having done his research, didn't mince words.

You're operating on the same budget as Williams, and our internal expectation is to finish in the top six. There's a real disconnect between what you want and what it actually takes to achieve it.

That meeting led to an offer. Mercedes wanted Toto to take over as head of Mercedes-Benz Motorsport and Team Principal of the F1 team. It was one of the most prestigious jobs in the industry, and he was honoured – but ownership had always been his model. He had never been a corporate employee. They smiled and said they had anticipated that answer.

You know the 40 per cent shareholding in the team owned by Aabar, the Abu Dhabi sovereign investment fund? They want to exit. We thought you could take over that shareholding.

When Toto came home and told me about it, there was no hesitation on my part. I knew – I just knew – he had to take this opportunity.

Of course, it wasn't that simple. We went into overdrive analysing the opportunity, risks and rewards. The investment team, the lawyers, tax consultants from various jurisdictions and M&A advisors crunched the numbers and started to structure what the transaction could look like.

Discussions went back and forth – Toto was never one to take blind risks. He had lost his father at fifteen after a long battle with brain cancer, and the family had endured severe financial hardship. The memory of losing everything as a child had left a deep imprint. For Toto, risk was something to be calculated, contained, never taken without knowing he could survive the worst-case scenario.

Toto also felt a deep loyalty to Frank and the people at Williams. That weighed heavily on him. But I was adamant. *You have to do this*, I kept telling him. He had the financial background, the private equity experience and, most importantly, the passion for racing. The more involved he had become at Williams, the more it was clear that he wasn't just a numbers guy – he had the energy, the vision and the drive to turn a team into something greater. Toto's influence at Williams was already being felt. And I knew that if he took this next step, he could do something even bigger.

The transaction took twelve months to piece together, layered with complexity. From my front-row seat, I watched the negotiations unfold, absorbing the countless ways a deal could be structured.

One task Mercedes left to Toto was informing their non-executive chairman, Niki Lauda, about the new structure and his revised role. Niki was a fellow Austrian and motorsport legend, but he and Toto weren't particularly close. Toto had tried to break Niki's lap record at the Nürburgring, and they'd discussed it at the time, but this new role would bring them into daily contact, and it felt important to Toto to let him know ahead of time. At the time, Niki had just orchestrated the high-profile signing of Lewis Hamilton to Mercedes – a seismic move in the sport.

Toto met Niki at a race and laid out the new situation, explaining that strict non-disclosure agreements had prevented him from sharing the details sooner. Niki was stunned and told Toto he needed twenty-four hours to process the news. But true to his direct and decisive nature, he was back within an hour.

Okay, you're an intelligent guy, I can understand the rationale, but I want in on the deal.

It was agreed that Niki would take a 10 per cent stake, leaving Toto with 30 per cent. Rather than contributing to legal fees, Niki proposed a different arrangement – Toto would fly with him to races on his private plane. The countless hours spent together in the air laid the foundation for what would become, over time, a deep and enduring friendship.

Initially, my own relationship with Niki was reserved; we had got off to a rocky start after our first meeting at DTM. However, as Toto and Niki worked more closely together, our relationship evolved naturally. I got the nickname Frau Susie and because Niki hated small talk and late nights, I would very often be his exit strategy.

We would love to stay longer but Frau Susie is very tired so we need to leave.

I would then, sometimes, mid-conversation, have to nod that, yes, I was feeling quite tired. That was Niki – straight to the point, never wasting words. And if there was one thing he had even less patience for than small talk, it was lateness. He ran on his own strict schedule and expected everyone else to do the same. We bonded over our joint efforts to get Toto running on time. If we were less than five minutes late, I would get a pat on the back. *Mission accomplished, Frau Susie.* Eventually, they agreed on a compromise – Niki took the early shift, Toto the late.

Finally, after months of back and forth, the deal was done and Toto had to tell Frank. He wrestled with deep conflict, feeling, in some way, that he was letting someone down that he held in the highest regard.

The day he was set to have the conversation, we were in England. Before he left for the factory, he told me, *This is going to be a really tough one.*

Just an hour later, he called.

Well? How did it go? I asked.

You're not going to believe this, he said, half laughing. *I spent ten minutes explaining everything – the opportunity, why it made sense for me, but also how difficult it was for me to come to this decision. Frank immediately asked if he could convince me to stay. I told him it was a tough decision, but my mind was made up. And do you know what he said next?*

I waited.

'*Well then, if that's the case, can I have a Mercedes engine?*'

I burst out laughing. That was Frank through and through – direct, always thinking about the team. He had been happy for Toto, of course, but he also had his eye on the bigger picture – getting a Mercedes engine for Williams. Classic Frank.

In January 2013, Toto became shareholder and Executive Director of the Mercedes Formula One team, marking the start of a whole new chapter in our lives. I was still with Williams, which meant that while we were both at the races, we each had our own paths, our own responsibilities. It was an unusual but perfect balance – we were in the same world, but we weren't following each other around.

Then came Silverstone. My moment. I would be taking to the track for the first practice session, replacing Valtteri Bottas and becoming the first woman in twenty-two years to take part in an F1 race weekend. The significance of the moment wasn't lost on me, but I wasn't out there to prove what a woman could achieve – I wanted to show I was quick, that I had the speed to deserve a chance to race in F1.

I asked French women's wear designer Roland Mouret, whose dresses I'd long admired and worn, to design a new race helmet. I wanted something different, a clear break from the usual masculine style. It was the first time a fashion designer had designed an F1 helmet, and what he delivered felt feminine, strong, and me.

We had chosen to stay in a motorhome at the circuit to avoid the usual traffic chaos on Friday morning. I didn't want anything distracting me. I was laser focused. That morning, we travelled to the track together. As we walked through the paddock, we reached the point where we had to split – me heading towards Williams, Toto continuing down the paddock to Mercedes. I stopped and turned to him.

Okay, see you later, I said.

He looked at me. *The next time I see you will be out on track in an F1 car.*

I nodded and waited for the words of encouragement, something reassuring or heartfelt. Instead, he just looked me dead in the eye and said, *Don't be shit.*

No fluff, no sentimentality. He had never wrapped me in cotton wool – he knew how brutal racing was, and that in the end, performance was all that mattered. And he knew exactly how to push me. In that moment, it worked. I smiled and walked away.

Don't be shit? Oh, I'll show you. Just wait.

By the time I climbed into the car, the sheer number of cameras pointed in my direction didn't even faze me. I was ready.

Then, on my first flying lap – my Mercedes engine blew up. Just like that, it was over. One lap.

All that anticipation, all that build-up, and in an instant it was gone. No chance to prove anything. Just crushing disappointment.

Andy Cowell, who was head of Mercedes' High-Performance Powertrains at the time, came over with Toto to see me in the Williams garage. He apologised – it was an oil pressure failure; he told me not to dwell on it. *You've got another chance in Hockenheim in a few weeks. Focus on that.*

And that was exactly what I did.

Hockenheim was my track. I knew it inside out. I told myself, *This is the one that counts.*

Two weeks later, I was back on track, and this time, I got to show what I could do. I ended the session just 0.2 seconds off Felipe Massa in the other Williams car.

It was the proudest moment of my career. Not just because I had taken to the track under the weight of so much expectation, knowing I couldn't crash, knowing I had to hand the car back intact. But because I had proved something real.

A woman could be competitive in Formula One.

13

HAVING done a strong job in free practice at Hockenheim and feeling so deeply embedded within the Williams team, I had hope. Maybe, just maybe, an opportunity would come my way. Realistically, it was a long shot. Williams had two strong drivers in Valtteri Bottas and Felipe Massa, so a full-time race seat wasn't a real possibility. But in Formula One, things can change in an instant. Opportunities arise when you least expect them. And so, despite the odds, I couldn't quite let go of the idea that something might open up.

There had been vague talks with one of the backmarker teams – Marussia at the time. They had made it clear: bring sponsorship and we'll put you in the car. Pay drivers have always been part of Formula One. The financial barrier to entry in the sport is massive, and at that time, the teams at the back of the grid were fighting just to survive. Every bit of sponsorship money could make the difference between staying on the grid or folding.

Despite the obvious marketing potential of a female driver in F1, it wasn't something that sponsors were rushing to support. There was still hesitation. I think, at that time, there was actually still a deep-seated reservation. A woman in Formula One hadn't been seen in decades, so much so that many people simply didn't believe it was possible. Women's sport as a whole hadn't yet reached the momentum it has today. There wasn't the same push, the same belief in female athletes as viable commercial properties. The tide was slowly starting to turn, but it wasn't moving fast enough.

But for me, it was simple – I wasn't going to put down money just to buy myself a race seat. Toto and I were completely aligned on that. If I was going to earn my place in Formula One, it had to be on my merit, not my money. So, despite my performance in the car, despite proving I could hold my own, the reality was that getting a race seat was still out of reach. However, at the opening race of the 2015 season in Melbourne came the news – Valtteri Bottas had suffered back pain during qualifying. After a medical assessment, he was transferred to the hospital and deemed unfit to take part in the race on Sunday.

My first thought was, of course, concern for Valtteri. I had known him for many years – Toto had managed him since he was an eighteen-year-old Finnish boy who had walked into his office, and he had been part of Toto's driver management company ever since. But my second thought came almost immediately after. Who's going to drive the car if Valtteri can't race at the next round? For the first time, I let myself believe – this could be my chance. Days later, Williams signed Adrian Sutil as the reserve driver.

That moment was a turning point. A moment of absolute clarity. If there had ever been a chance for me to step up into a race seat, this had been it. And if they weren't willing to put me in the car now, they never would.

I wasn't going to sit on the sidelines as a marketing tool. I had driven the car. I had put in the work. I had proven myself. I was grateful for the opportunities I'd had, but I wasn't about to keep showing up at races, doing sponsor events, and playing a role that wasn't leading me towards the grid. I went to see Pat Symonds, who was the Technical Director at the time, and I told him outright how devastated I was that they had chosen Adrian Sutil – someone with no connection to the team – when I had been there, doing the work, preparing for exactly this kind of moment. I had done a full pre-season test in Barcelona the previous year. I had completed a full race distance and ended up fifth on the timing sheets. I had done FP1 at Hockenheim. I had proved I was capable. His response was blunt.

You've never done a race, and we want someone in the car with experience.

And that was it. That was the moment I knew – this chapter was over. If they weren't going to give me the opportunity to get experience, it was never going to happen. Williams offered me another year as a test driver. But by then, I had already made my decision.

I was thirty-three. As a racing driver, as an athlete, you always know that your sporting career will end eventually. And I had always been determined to be in control of my own destiny. I wasn't going to wait until my performance started to slip, until my phone stopped ringing, until someone else made the decision for me. I wanted to leave on my terms. While I was at my peak. While I still had something to give.

I wasn't interested in just fading into the background as an ex-racing driver. I wanted to build something. I wanted to be successful in whatever I chose to do next. So the decision to step away from racing was, in the end, an easy one. It was formally announced at the end of the season that I would be ending my racing career.

I knew that I wanted to give something back. Throughout my career, I had only ever done one interview where I wasn't asked about my gender. The fact that it was so rare said everything about the state of the sport.

What's more, there had been a moment earlier in the year that had truly opened my eyes to the broader reality of my presence in Formula One. After my run at Silverstone, the head of aerodynamics at Williams approached me with a story about his daughter. As they watched the session, she was playing with her dolls on the floor near the television. When she saw me remove my helmet, she turned to her father and asked in disbelief, *That's a girl?*

He nodded. *Yes, Susie is our test driver. She's driving in the first practice session for Williams today at the British Grand Prix.*

Her response stunned him: *But how? Girls aren't allowed to drive in F1.*

The fact that a little girl whose own father worked in the industry didn't even believe it was possible was a stark reminder of how deeply ingrained these perceptions were. I knew that if things were ever going to change, I had to drive that change. I wanted to make sure I passed the baton to the next generation – to open up the sport and show that success was possible for women, both on track and off.

That's how my initiative Dare to be Different was born. I had been included in a *Vanity Fair* feature on women who 'Dare to be Different' and that inspired the name. I set it up in partnership with the governing body of British motorsport, Motorsport UK. The idea was simple but powerful – to challenge the preconception that motorsport was a man's world. Because at the time, it still very much was.

I had always been held up as an example of what could be possible, but I wanted to go beyond that. I wanted to actively create opportunities for young girls to get hands-on experience in the sport – to drive a kart for the first time, to understand what it's like to be a mechanic, or even to work as a journalist covering a race. Formula One wasn't the global phenomenon it is now. It wasn't as commercially dominant, and the visibility of women in motorsport was almost non-existent. Dare to be Different was one of the first real efforts to change that.

At the same time, Michèle Mouton was leading the FIA's Women in Motorsport Commission. She was someone I had always deeply respected – the only woman to have won not just one but four World Rally Championship rallies, ending up as vice Rally World Champion in 1982. An incredible feat.

We shared the same beliefs about how to get more women into the sport. For both of us, it was never about tokenism. It wasn't about getting more girls into motorsport just for the sake of it. It was about performance. It was about doing things the right way. We wanted women to be given opportunities, but we also believed that they had to earn their way up. Michèle and I had countless conversations, and as Dare to be Different started to gain momentum, she was keen for us to join forces.

For me, it was never about ownership or personal accolades – it was about making an impact. So when the opportunity came to integrate Dare to be Different into the FIA, I didn't hesitate. Dare to be Different evolved into FIA Girls on Track, a global initiative that runs to this day. Off the back of that work, I was awarded an MBE for services to women's sport, but more importantly, Mum finally got her graduation picture for the kitchen wall, as I was awarded an Honorary Degree from Edinburgh University.

After setting up Dare to be Different, I naturally started thinking about what would come next. By that time, Toto was having huge success in Formula One, and I was incredibly proud of him. But that was his success, and I wanted to achieve my own – to continue to contribute to our marriage in my own right. As exciting as it was to have a blank sheet of paper in front of me, it was also daunting and I started to feel an emptiness creeping in.

What did I actually want to do? Where was this next chapter leading me?

Again, I leaned heavily on my gut instinct.

*　　*　　*

My world was still deeply intertwined with Toto's. Mercedes were dominating F1, achieving thirty-four victories out of a possible thirty-eight over two seasons. He thrived under the immense pressure but didn't lose his ease. He often said, *It's the long game that counts, not where we find ourselves at half time.* Our feet stayed firmly on the ground, and continuing to act with humility was at the core of his values.

His relentless focus was on the collective success. To him, the trophies and accolades belonged equally to those behind the scenes. He deliberately started sending team members onto the podium to collect trophies, visibly sharing the spotlight, a first for a Team Principal and an act that is now common in F1. He always said, *When you stand on the podium, you're standing on the shoulders of the 2,500 people behind you.*

I often watched him and thought, *He makes it look easy – but it's anything but.* He often recalled his days working as an instructor, like me, dreaming of a life in racing. He had worked at the Walter Lechner Racing School in Spielberg where the Austrian GP took place, and it was on our drive back to his hometown of Vienna after the Austrian GP in 2014 that gave us a moment of real reflection. It was a Mercedes 1-2 but with Valtteri, who Toto had managed, in P3 for Williams and Felipe Massa in P4. At the time we still owned shares in both teams, and we had a feeling of gratitude and appreciation for just how far the journey had taken us.

I decided to join the commentating team for Channel 4's Formula One coverage. On the surface, it was an easy decision. I would still be travelling to race weekends, still immersed in the world I loved, and I'd be able to spend time with Toto. People often assume those weekends were glamorous, but the reality was far from it. Sometimes we were so exhausted by the end of the day that we'd get back to the hotel, barely speak, just enjoy the silence, and order room service. But just being together made all the difference.

There was one pre-production meeting that still makes me laugh. The whole crew was there, going through the rundown for the programme. At one point, Eddie Jordan was scheduled to do an interview with Toto, and the director started outlining the plan for the segment.

Eddie cut him off. *Oh, I'm going to go for it. Don't you worry,* he said, launching into a full-blown rant about how he was going to really go after Toto, ask him the toughest questions, put him under pressure.

Then, suddenly, the room fell completely silent.

Nobody made eye contact. People started glancing down at the floor, a few side-eyes flicking in my direction.

Eddie, still mid-rant, finally clocked what was happening. His expression shifted. He looked at me, realising – Oh, shit. She's in the room.

I just met his eyes, deadpan, and said, *Go for it, Eddie. Go get him.*

The room erupted in laughter.

Toto often asked me to come along even to races where I wouldn't be working but I always hesitated.

You're so busy, I'd tell him. *I can't just sit around all day.*

There were two main reasons for that. First, I couldn't stand the feeling of being surrounded by people who were so driven, so focused, so busy – while I had no clear purpose for being there. And second, I knew I'd end up eating way too much because the food in the Mercedes hospitality was so good and never stopped coming – my willpower didn't stand a chance.

That was part of the appeal of the commentary role. It gave me something to do on race weekends, a sense of structure and involvement. And I enjoyed it. The camaraderie between the commentators, the energy of being trackside, the thrill of the race weekends. But I also quickly realised something: I didn't want to commentate on other people's successes or failures. I wanted to be the one achieving something. For me, anyone who puts themselves in the ring – whether they win or lose – deserves respect. The real challenge is in doing, in taking that risk. And I wanted to be taking risks. I wanted to be pushing for something of my own.

Many people presumed I'd stepped away from racing to become a mother. The constant stream of predictable questions about the path society expected women to follow bored me. When are you getting married? Then immediately after marriage, when are you having children? I'd never been someone who felt motherhood was an essential part of my identity. I didn't retire from racing to start a family. My bond with Rosi and Benedict had already given me a meaningful experience of motherhood, and I felt no urgent need to experience it firsthand.

But around this time, Toto and I sat down and talked about

it. It wasn't some grand decision – it was more of a casual conversation, a shared thought that perhaps it was something that we wanted. Without overthinking it, I made an appointment with my doctor. I had put my body through so much over the years – intense training, relentless travel, the physical demands of racing. I knew, realistically, that getting pregnant might not be straightforward.

After running some tests, the doctor was honest with me. *Look, let's try naturally for a couple of years. If nothing happens, we can look at options, an operation to improve your chances.*

I remember sitting there, nodding, feeling totally at ease. There was no rush, no pressure. I called Toto after the appointment and told him exactly that – if it happens, great; if it doesn't, that's okay too. We had Rosi and Benedict. We were extremely happy. There was no sense of urgency.

Six weeks later, I was pregnant. I walked back into the doctor's office, and as soon as she saw me, she frowned. *We've just seen each other recently, is there a problem?*

You said it could take up to two years . . .

She shook her head. *There's no way you're already pregnant.*

I laughed. *Yes, there is.*

I know how challenging it can be for some women to conceive, and looking back, I'm profoundly grateful that it happened so naturally for me. My pregnancy was smooth, and I cherished those months. Life continued as usual – I travelled to races with Toto, and during the summer shutdown in August, just past my twelfth week of pregnancy, we went downhill mountain biking. Riding with a group, we approached a rocky stretch of trail. As I leaned back, trying to absorb the rough terrain, my bike hit a deep rabbit hole. Suddenly, I was launched over the handlebars, somersaulting down the steep slope.

I was fine – I knew I was fine. But before I could even dust myself off, Toto had already flung his bike to the ground and sprinted up to me in a panic. *Are you okay? Is everything okay?*

Normally, if I took a fall, his reaction would be the complete opposite – something along the lines of, *Get up, come on, you're fine.* But this time, there was real concern in his face. The rest of the group, who were already waiting at the bottom and obviously didn't know I was pregnant, just stared at him. They weren't used to seeing that side of Toto – so openly protective, so different from his usual just get on with it attitude.

I looked up at him, completely unbothered. *I'm fine*, I said. *Really. Don't worry.*

He stared at me for another second, scanning me for any sign of injury, before finally exhaling. And then, with a little shake of his head, he muttered, *Only you would go mountain biking while pregnant.*

That time was just wonderful. Maybe it was the hormones, maybe it was just the shift in pace, but I was happy. I remember afternoons where I'd sit down, thinking I just needed a short rest – then I'd wake up three hours later. It was the first time in my life that I had truly relaxed. I wasn't thinking about my next career move, about what came next. I was going to become a mother, and I wanted to be fully present for those first months. No stress, no pressure – just time to prepare, to enjoy the moment.

Of course, as my pregnancy progressed, things became a little less comfortable. The bigger I got, the more my body felt alien to me. Not being able to train properly, not feeling as fit and strong as I usually did – that was a challenge. I also refused to buy maternity clothes. Instead, I just bought normal clothes in bigger sizes, reasoning that I wasn't going to be this size for long.

Our baby was due in April, around the Chinese and Bahrain Grands Prix. It was too risky to leave it to chance, so I decided to have a planned Caesarean to make sure Toto could be there. I was at home in Switzerland and would be having the baby in Zurich. The day before the scheduled Caesarean, I went into the hospital for routine checks while Toto was still making his way back from China.

I was lying in the hospital room, getting checked over, when the kind nurse left me for a moment. When she returned, she had a curious look on her face.

We're seeing some contractions, she said.

I don't feel anything, I replied.

Are you sure? Because we're clearly seeing something.

No, I feel nothing, I insisted.

She looked uncertain. *When is your husband arriving?*

Not until tomorrow morning, I said. *And I absolutely want him to be here.*

She hesitated before saying, *Well, my advice is to stay as still as possible so we can proceed with the planned Caesarean tomorrow.*

And that was all I needed to hear. I did not move a single muscle that evening and called Toto. Flustered, he said, *I'm on my way, but I'm halfway over China at the moment!*

Of course, despite the slight panic, the overwhelming emotion was excitement – our baby was nearly here.

Everything in Switzerland is precise, down to the minute, and that morning, I had nothing to do but wait. I was scheduled for my Caesarean at midday, and the hospital had everything under control. But I was restless, so I decided to drive to the airport and pick up Toto myself.

When he walked out and spotted me sitting there in the car, he looked utterly surprised.

What the hell are you doing here?

I was so bored that I decided to come and collect you myself, I said, as if it were the most normal thing in the world.

He laughed, hugged me, and we drove back to the hospital together. I was eager to hear all about the race weekend. He talked, I listened, and for a little while, everything felt completely normal. Once we arrived, they started getting me ready for surgery. I was lying in bed, prepped and waiting, when Toto turned to me.

Do you think I have time to dial into my debrief from the Chinese Grand Prix?

I laughed. *Absolutely. Go for it.*

To be honest, I was just as interested to hear what had happened in the race. Lewis had won but Ferrari was starting to fight back and had won the opening race of the season. So there I was, already in my hospital gown, and there was

Toto – sitting on the sofa, coffee in hand, fully immersed in his post-race debrief. Then, at quarter to twelve, the doctor walked in.

Right, are we ready? It's time to go now.

Toto nodded, still on the call.

Yes, Mr Wolff, your baby is just about to be born, the doctor added, a hint of amusement in his voice. *Are you coming?*

Toto looked up, smiled, and said, *Oh, of course.* Then, back to the call – *Listen, guys, I have to go because, well, my son's about to be born.*

There was a flurry of congratulations on the other end of the line before he hung up, put on his gown and walked with me as I was wheeled down to the theatre. And just minutes later, Jack – our little Jacky boy – was with us.

Toto stayed for two days before he had to fly to Bahrain for the next Grand Prix. My mum and dad were there along with Toto's mother, and those early weeks were just pure joy, to soak in every moment and to fall completely in love with our little boy.

I had chosen not to go to any pre-natal classes so I didn't really know what was coming, but I figured I'd just deal with it when the time came. Toto, however, wasn't comfortable with the idea of me being left alone once Mum and Dad had to go back to Scotland, so we had an Italian maternity nurse, Maria, come to stay. She was wonderful, and I was completely over-whelmed with love and happiness.

Despite the feeling of content, towards the end of the year, something slowly started to shift. A restlessness. I loved being with Jack, but I couldn't shake the feeling that I was still capable of achieving more. I started thinking about the life I wanted Jack to see. His dad was accomplishing so much, and I had grown up watching my own parents build things, push themselves, go out into the world and do something. I wanted Jack to see me doing that too. I remember joining Toto at a sponsor dinner. The person next to me asked, *So, what do you do?*

And I just sat there, caught totally off guard. *What do I do?*

For the first time in my life, I had no answer. And suddenly, I was in freefall. I didn't know who I was anymore. I had completely lost my sense of identity. What did I want the second stage of my life to look like?

I knew that I wanted quality time with my family. That was when I was at my happiest. But at the same time, I had too much fire inside me. I had too much drive to sit still. And I remembered a conversation I'd had the day I left hospital with Jack.

The head of the maternity unit had come to say goodbye. She was in her early sixties, a midwife for decades. Before I left, she said, *You're going to hear so much advice in the next few weeks as a new mother. But if there's one thing you should remember, it's this – if you're happy, your baby will be happy.*

At the time, I had smiled, nodded, not really thinking much of it.

But a few months later, those words started ringing so true.

I had to be happy. The idea that I was going to just stop – to give up everything, to put aside my ambitions – suddenly felt inconceivable.

I had to do something.

When I first found out I was pregnant, Toto was absolutely overjoyed. We both were. But he also said something that, at the time, I didn't fully understand.

Please, I don't want to lose you. I don't want to lose my wife, my best friend and my sparring partner.

I remember thinking, lose me? What does he mean? It didn't make sense, so I brushed it aside. But now, I did understand. And I wasn't worried about Toto losing me – I was worried about losing myself. In those early months, I was totally consumed by motherhood. Jack was everything, my whole focus. But somewhere along the way, I started to feel like I had lost myself, like I was no longer in the driver's seat of my own life. And that feeling was unsettling. I had always needed a purpose, a challenge, something to fight for, but if I was going to leave Jack, if I was going to split my focus, then whatever I did had to be meaningful. It had to matter.

It was a challenging time. I remember reading constantly whenever Jack was asleep, or in the quiet evenings while Toto was away, grasping at anything that might offer guidance. Biographies, books on growth and finding purpose – some felt overly simplistic, but they resonated with me. I needed something to hold onto, something to help me find my way forward.

I started looking at opportunities through the family investment office, discussing possibilities with René. I explored the idea of investing in fashion – Roland Mouret was looking for investors and it was something different. For a while, I seriously considered stepping into that world. But the more I researched, the more I realised – I knew nothing about the industry. And it was tough to make the numbers work.

Then I looked into wellness. The rise of boutique fitness franchises, the surge in supplements and health-conscious brands – it was a booming space, but again, it didn't feel right.

Around that time I got a call from a gentleman called Gildo Pastor. He owned a Formula E team in the newly formed all-electric championship and his family had made their fortune in Monégasque real estate. We had met a couple of years before when he had approached me to drive for his team but I was a complete cynic about electric racing. I didn't see the appeal. Formula E? Battery-powered race cars? I couldn't imagine it ever being a thing.

I assumed he was going to ask me – again – to drive one of his cars. But instead, he said something that took me by surprise.

I don't want you to drive, Susie. I want you to run my team.

I actually laughed.

Run a Formula E team? It felt so far removed from where I was at that moment that I couldn't even take it seriously. Managing a team wasn't something I had ever considered. It wasn't part of the plan – I had mentally decided I wouldn't work in motorsport. I didn't want to work for Toto, for the sake of our marriage, and I didn't want to work against Toto, for the sake of our marriage. So it was a firm thank you but no thank you.

I remember how, in the middle of all this uncertainty, a

few people said to me, *Oh, you're just dealing with postnatal depression.*

That infuriated me.

How easily they had put a label on what I was feeling – because if a woman has a baby and then feels lost, well, it must be postnatal depression, right?

But I knew my body. I knew myself. And I knew it wasn't depression.

It was a feeling of being lost.

Looking back now, I see how easily people jump to conclusions, how quick they are to diagnose, to explain away something complex with a single word. The reality was, I was going through a huge adjustment. There was this little person who needed me constantly, who had become the centre of my world. And yet, I was still trying to hold onto the person I had been – the ambition, the drive, the hunger to achieve something beyond motherhood.

I had spoken openly about my struggles to a couple of close friends in Austria – Claudia, who I had known and worked with since my early racing days, and Anita, who ran the Wings for Life foundation and was a mother herself. Her former partner was Dietrich Mateschitz, the founder of Red Bull.

Anita immediately sympathised.

I know exactly what you're going through.

And in our long discussions she told me something that had really helped her.

A seminar.

*   *   *

I hesitated. I wasn't against self-help: I enjoyed books that helped me navigate ways through things – but a seminar? A room where people might be asked to hug, share things with total strangers? It felt unlikely.

Things carried on as they were, but the idea of the seminar lingered. It nagged away at me. Anita was on my wavelength so I eventually came to the conclusion I should at least give it a try.

My worst fears were confirmed when I arrived at the seminar and the first thing we were asked to do was give the person next to us a hug. *Turn to the person on your left and give them a hug! Now turn to the person on your right and give them a hug!*

I looked at the person to my left. *Absolutely not.*

I turned to the person on my right. *We are not hugging.*

At that moment, I was contemplating just walking out.

But I was already there. Mum and Dad had come from Scotland especially to look after Jack. If I walked out now, I'd just feel foolish. *See it through*, I told myself. By the end of the first day, I wasn't hugging anyone, but I was starting to absorb what was happening in the room. Over the next couple of days, things began to shift. The seminar was focused on putting yourself in the best possible position for success. It began to click – I wasn't doing that for myself: my current situation wasn't setting me up for anything. But it was only on the third day, when the concept of modelling the success of others was introduced, that I realised how I could change things. The idea was simple when broken down: find someone who has the kind of success that inspires you. Then dissect exactly what they did to get there.

What did they do differently? What set them apart?

And in the best-case scenario, if it was someone within reach, ask them to mentor you. Learn from them directly.

Who inspired me?

Who had achieved unprecedented success that I admired?

I sat there scribbling notes, and then suddenly, the answer hit me.

This person had started with nothing and become hugely successful.

Had gone on to rewrite the Formula One history books.

I had a front-row seat to their success.

Reach out and ask them to mentor me?

I woke up next to him nearly every single morning. My husband, Toto.

Just like that, the fog lifted. I wasn't stuck. I just hadn't been able to see what was right in front of me. I knew where I needed to go and what I needed to do.

I stood up, walked straight out, pulled out my phone, and messaged Gildo Pallanca Pastor.

Let's talk.

Gildo was a visionary, becoming a pioneering expert in electric mobility long before electric cars became mainstream and breaking multiple electric land speed records. The Formula E Championship had been founded by Alejandro Agag, a charismatic Spanish entrepreneur who had once been a politician before turning his hand to motorsport.

I had gradually started hearing more about the growing potential of electrification. And then Dieselgate, the Volkswagen emissions scandal, happened and almost overnight the automotive industry was forced to accelerate its transition to electric. What had seemed like a slow, distant evolution was suddenly happening at an unstoppable pace. The momentum behind electrification was undeniable. It was gaining traction, and starting to get some serious attention.

We agreed to meet in Paris and Gildo laid out his vision for his Formula E team. The team was struggling, stuck at the back of the grid and losing a lot of money. He had gone through some serious health issues, which meant he was forced to take a back seat, and now he doubted the management in place. And yet, despite only knowing me from those brief moments when he'd tried to convince me to drive for him, he was now asking me to run his team.

It was a bold offer.

I arrived home that evening, and Toto was keen to hear how the meeting had gone.

I'm going to go for it, I said. *I'm going to be Team Principal. I believe I can turn it around and make it successful again.*

Toto didn't hesitate. *You absolutely can – go for it.* And then a brief pause. *But don't just become the Team Principal. Have skin in the game. Copy my deal – take 30 per cent equity.*

And that was it.

I went back into the family investment office, sat down with

René, and we pulled apart all the details of how they had structured the Mercedes deal. I copied and pasted the playbook. But the team was at the back of the grid, losing $11 million a year. We agreed that I wouldn't take a salary, but instead, equity.

By the time it was finalised, I wasn't just the Team Principal of Venturi Formula E – I was a 30 per cent shareholder.

In July 2018, just over a year after Jack was born, I walked into my first press conference.

A media roundtable, cameras ready, microphones placed in front of me.

The first question:

What qualifies you for this job?

Fair enough. *There are many ex-racing drivers who go on to run teams*, I replied. *I believe I can do the job.*

The second question:

Did your husband get you the job?

I looked straight at them. *No, he didn't.*

The third question:

You've just had a baby – how are you going to manage the travel and the running of a team now that you're a mother?

This sport had obviously not evolved very much since I stopped racing.

But I'd been here before – I knew exactly what to do. Focus on performance, turn this team around and make it a success. Then nobody – absolutely nobody – would talk about me being the only female Team Principal in Formula E.

14

WAS eager to get started. The team was based in Monaco, but relocating was never an option. We were settled in Switzerland and our family base couldn't just be uprooted. When I discussed this with Gildo, he didn't hesitate.

I won't judge how you do it, he said. *You know what needs to be done – do it your way.*

He had put his full trust in me and it gave me the confidence to approach the role on my terms. I decided that I'd work remotely, make regular trips to the office, and travel to every test and race.

None of it would have been possible without my parents. When I told them about my plans, their response was immediate: total support. They would be there whenever I needed them, ready to step in and look after Jack. That reassurance was everything. I'd always had some help with childcare, but I never liked being away from Jack for more than a night as he was so young. This challenge was only feasible because I had that rock-solid foundation of family behind me.

Before taking over officially, I went to the final race of the previous season – unannounced, quietly observing. It was clear that Venturi wasn't taken seriously due to their lack of results. In the paddock, we were seen as an afterthought, a struggling backmarker. But as I stood in Brooklyn, the Statue of Liberty in the distance and electric race cars racing through the streets, I knew it had the potential to be something big. Electrification wasn't yet mainstream, but momentum was building, fuelled by regulation, new technology and changing consumer tastes, with Tesla's first model showing that electric cars could be fast as well as stylish.

Many automotive manufacturers were beginning to publicly commit to an electric future, and I was stepping in at exactly the right moment: Formula E had just introduced its new 'Generation 2' design, which for the first time carried enough battery range to complete a full race distance. Until then, drivers had been forced to swap cars mid-race when the battery ran out – a limitation seen as emblematic of the shortcomings of electric vehicles. Now, the rapid pace of development made Formula E a showcase for just how quickly the technology was evolving.

After my announcement, I travelled to Monaco for the first time to meet the team. I spent those early days sitting in meetings, mostly listening, absorbing everything. I wasn't an engineer, and I had never driven an electric racing car. I wanted to be clear on that with everyone from the start. But I knew how a racing car functioned, and I was determined to understand this new technology.

Unlike F1 or most racing cars, a Formula E car runs entirely on battery power. There is no petrol, no engine and no exhaust.

Just an electric motor powered by lithium batteries with a lower top speed but instant acceleration, going from 0 to 100 kilometres per hour in under three seconds. With no engine, there is also no sound. Replacing the normal roar of an engine was a high-pitched whine. In a nod to sustainability, like a road car, there was only one type of tyre that would be used for both dry and wet running. Similar to F1 cars they also used regenerative braking: when the driver hits the brakes, the car actually recovers some of that energy and recharges the battery, the equivalent of getting a little bit of fuel each time you slow down. Energy management during a race would replace tyre and pit stop strategies. I pored over every detail – where the marginal gains might emerge, from optimal regeneration under braking to software mapping that maximised the flow of power between battery and motor, throttle mapping, battery temperature control, and the simulation tools that let us manage energy across different race tracks and conditions.

It was obvious that if we were going to turn things around, I needed the right people in place. Having team members who were known and successful would give us more credibility. I started by mapping out our current structure, then spent time on LinkedIn researching who was in which position in which team and how the most successful teams at the front of the grid were structured. Motorsport is a world where knowledge is power, and often the fastest way to gain an advantage is by bringing in talent from winning teams – people who already know what it takes to be at the top.

One name kept coming up – a French engineer who had

just won the championship the previous season. Through a contact, I managed to set up a call. The response was cautious: *He's happy to speak with you, but don't expect him to join.*

I knew it was a long shot, it would all come down to the pitch. I shared my vision, not just for where the team could go, but for who we could become, and how I planned to restructure the technical organisation and bring in the best people for every role. He would be part of that transformation, an architect of our reinvention. We were agile, open, and I made one thing clear: failure wasn't an option. He'd already reached the top with his driver – now was the time to show what he could do with a team chasing its very first win. At the end of the call, he said he'd think about it.

By the end of the day, he called back. *I'm in.*

That was the first key hire and I was fired up. Bringing someone so highly rated on board was a statement to the wider paddock that we meant business. Restructuring the technical team was a massive task, but his arrival gave us an insight into what it took to win. And sure enough, by making that first key hire, more were inclined to join us. I then secured a new chief engineer – someone I had highly rated from Formula Three. Piece by piece, we built a core group of people who respected each other, were open with each other and shared one burning ambition: to take Venturi from an afterthought to a real contender. These were engineers who were used to winning. They saw the challenge, and they were ready to rise to it.

But no matter how strong our technical team was, we needed the right drivers in the cars – they were the last line of attack. Gildo had already signed Felipe Massa before my arrival and he brought clout given his F1 track record with Ferrari, and popularity. In the other car I was keen to keep a very fast Swiss driver called Edo Mortara; he was fast – capable of winning races, even championships – but he didn't believe the team could fight at the front. He was already looking for a way out when I arrived and was speaking to other front-running teams. We sat down together and discussed all the areas in which the team was weak. I knew I had to make him part of the journey, make him believe that our trajectory was strong. I gave him the same message – we were building a team to bring Venturi back to the front. Edo agreed to stay.

On the operational side, I had a mountain to climb. In those early months, there were moments when I thought, *What have I got myself into?* Unlike a Formula One team, where each department had its own management structure, Venturi was still growing and had just twenty-four team members, which meant I had to have a grasp on every area of the business. Since it was a smaller organisation with a lower budget, every-one had to take on multiple roles. The scale of the task felt immense and I was completely out of my comfort zone. I had no choice but to learn fast and I knew I needed exceptional people around me. I took the approach of hiring the best and empowering them.

Then there were the contracts. Stacks of them. Not only did I have to read through each one to grasp our situation, but it became clear that some were heavily skewed against us. We had a Monégasque law firm handling our legal affairs, but it didn't take long to realise they didn't fully understand motorsport. And motorsport contracts, whether technical agreements, sponsorship deals or driver contracts, are uniquely complex, often with finely worded clauses related to team performance which could trigger exit clauses. I needed someone with deep industry knowledge.

That's when I brought in Anastasia. I had come across her while running Dare to be Different, and she was sharp and highly efficient. A mother of three, fiercely passionate about motorsport, she soon became an invaluable ally. I remember countless evenings where we were online combing through contracts and one of us would say, *I need to put my son to bed*, and the other would reply, *Me too – let's regroup after.* And we did, picking up calls late into the night once our children were asleep.

Those months were relentless. I travelled to Monaco every couple of weeks, bringing Jack with me along with a nanny. I'd sleep in the same room as him, enjoy the few hours of calm when he woke, then head to the office, put him to bed in the evening, and then go straight back to the office. Often, I wouldn't leave until two or three in the morning. No one was forcing me to work those hours – it was my choice. I've never been the type to switch off when there's unfinished business. If there's a job to be done, I have to see it through.

Over the course of my first year, I had built the most diverse team in Formula E, with a third of the workforce being female. I was proud of that, but that was never the goal. You don't earn points for diversity. It all comes down to performance. What mattered was creating an environment where people were empowered to do their best work. For the women on my team, that often meant finding a way to balance work and motherhood in a way motorsport rarely accommodated. As one of the only female leaders in high-level motorsport, I wanted to lead by example. To show that it could be done differently, that top-performing women who were often not considered for certain roles could be given the chance in the right circumstances. One example was my team manager, Delphine.

She was brilliant, highly capable and integral to Venturi. With an engineering background and experience at Williams F1, she had been with the team since the beginning. Within my first few months at Venturi, she asked for a meeting and promptly handed me her resignation letter. She was going through a divorce, facing the challenge of shared custody, and, despite loving her job, couldn't see how she could continue travelling while managing life as a single mother.

I wasn't willing to lose her – not because she was the only female team manager in Formula E but because she was one of the best. I told her I wasn't accepting her resignation and asked how we could make it work. We went through every option. Could her parents help? Her in-laws? I told her we'd figure it out together. And we did, making small adjustments to her travel schedule which allowed her some flexibility to leave a day later to the race weekends and return home on a Sunday evening. Delphine stayed and today she's my Head of Race Operations at F1 Academy.

The same approach was extended across the team. I had managed to hire Liz, an exceptional woman with F1 experience, to manage all of our PR and communications, as well as the women in marketing and partnerships, nearly all of whom were mothers. I never questioned if they had to step away for a school appointment or work from home when their child was sick. I knew what it was like to juggle everything, and I didn't care where they worked from – only that they got the job done and did it well. I applied the same standards to myself, balancing work between home and the office, managing my own travel schedule. This was before the pandemic changed the concept of how we work, but that culture of trust and empowerment allowed people to thrive, and in the end, that was why we built such a diverse and high-performing team.

Another challenge in Formula E is timing. Unlike Formula One, Formula E races are packed into a single day. With our circuits built in city centres through the normal streets, the disruption to traffic means there's no room for multi-day events. Everything has to happen fast. The Formula E seasons run mid-year to mid-year, taking us to some of the most iconic cities in the world – Paris, Hong Kong, Monaco, New York, Rome – to name a few.

Races started early – sometimes requiring us to be at the circuit as early as 4.30 a.m. – and in certain locations, the cold was brutal at that hour. Once the chill set in, I'd struggle to shake it for the rest of the day, even when the sun finally broke through. So I adapted. Heat patches on my back became a ritual, a way to fight off the cold before it settled deep. My ski thermals were another essential, hidden under my team kit.

With the timetable so condensed, preparation and precision were everything. There was no room for error – if you hit a problem or lost track time in the morning, the race could unravel before it even began.

That was my domain: organisation, preparation, setting a standard. We weren't a big manufacturer team with endless resources, but I drilled into everyone that we didn't need the most extravagant garage – we needed the most disciplined one. Attention to detail became non-negotiable. No half-empty plastic water bottles cluttering our engineering briefings. No disorganised workspaces. Everything had to be immaculate, not for vanity but because precision leads to performance. The marginal gains can make the difference between winning or not. And on race day, the smallest details often made the biggest difference.

Race weekends typically kicked off with a Team Principals' meeting the day before. Formula E management would present updates and teams would voice concerns. At my very first meeting, the session began with, *Good morning, gentlemen*, until one Team Principal raised his hand and said, *Excuse me, but we now have Susie in the room. We need to change our greeting.*

I found it amusing rather than offensive. I wasn't there to be a token inclusion and they knew that. I had my place in the room, and I was welcomed without hesitation. Many of the Team Principals were familiar faces from my racing days. But what fascinated me most, after attending a few meetings, was watching the dynamics unfold – the egos, the alliances, the carefully crafted arguments. Some loved the sound of their own voice, others played a long game. I saw no need to speak unless I had something meaningful to contribute. Instead, I focused on understanding the politics – who was aligned with whom, which teams were pushing for rule changes and, most importantly, why.

Manufacturers and customer teams had different agendas, and every proposed tweak to a sporting or technical regulation had a ripple effect. The key was thinking two steps ahead – better yet, five. That was something I'd learned from watching Toto, who never made a move without considering the full chessboard.

The race days themselves were brutal. Unlike Formula One, where the paddock is a permanent fixture, Formula E was built on temporary structures. More often than not, we were operating out of a glorified tent. It was raw and intense. But I thrived.

I didn't have an office. Most of the time, I'd be perched on a freight box at the back of the garage, making calls, having meetings, and dealing with whatever fire needed putting out next. Every problem, in every area of the team, ultimately landed with me. In the early days, before we had our systems fully dialled in, it often felt like pure firefighting. I had to figure out my own strategies for making it through the day.

I remember one particular race weekend where it was just one thing after another – relentless. At some point, I realised the only solitude I was going to get was in the toilet. But instead of actually using it, I just shut off the light, sat in the darkness and set a timer for five minutes. Five minutes of silence before I took a deep breath, opened the door and walked straight back into the chaos.

I also learned to say no – and then I got really good at it. In a high-pressure environment, you have to set boundaries. You can't go to every event, and you don't need to. Yes, I missed out on some valuable networking opportunities and a few glamorous nights, but time is limited, and I had to be disciplined with how I spent it.

A lot of people assumed I'd try to copy Toto, that I'd run to him every time I hit a roadblock. Of course, I valued his opinion – he had multiple World Championships behind him, and I deeply respected the way he managed his team, his people, and the sheer level of compassion he had for them. But I also knew I wasn't Toto. I had to find my own way of leading.

Venturi had a deeply French culture, shaped by its Monaco base. Communication wasn't always open. In my experience, the French can be quite reserved, and while I didn't speak the language, I also had to remember that English wasn't their first language. People would nod along during meetings, only for frustrations to explode afterwards when someone disagreed with a decision. That had to change.

We just couldn't afford to shy away from confrontation; we were a small team, and resentment was a dead weight. I pushed for a culture where people spoke up in the room, not behind closed doors. There was no value in pointing fingers when we lost a race or when a detail had been missed. The focus had to be on understanding why mistakes happened and how we'd stop them from happening again. I spent time figuring out where relationships within the team were strong, where they broke down, and where unspoken tensions were slowing us down. If someone had a problem with another team member, we sat down and hashed it out. I had no patience for politics. If there was an issue, it needed to be addressed – not left to fester.

I didn't have much management experience when I started at Venturi, but I had to become comfortable quickly with asserting my authority.

There was no space for hesitation or missteps. In racing, there's only one measure that matters – the stopwatch. The results would tell me, without question, whether I was making the right decisions behind the scenes.

And they did. We built momentum – and in motorsport, momentum and confidence are everything. Not just for the drivers but for the entire team. A fourth place in Santiago, then on to Mexico, where we stood on the podium. And then came Hong Kong.

The track was built out on the port, the skyline towering in the background. It was fitting that one of the most fast-paced, high-energy cities in the world would have such a dramatic course. We were viewed as real competitors now; and we were ready to win.

We didn't cross the line first. We finished second, but the

race winner was penalised for forcing another car off track. Just like that, the victory was ours. I called Gildo from the podium – we were race winners. This win felt different from my successes as a driver. It wasn't just mine. It was ours. No longer was I a lone competitor focused only on myself; this was a triumph for the entire team. We had made history – the first and only Monégasque racing team to win. And when we returned home, we were celebrated.

It was validation that we were moving in the right direction. We were no longer an afterthought – we were in the fight. A breakthrough moment, in a place that never stops moving. It felt like we'd only go up from there.

Then came the Rome Grand Prix. Both our cars were in the top ten, and it looked like another breakthrough weekend. The customer team we supplied with electric powertrains had both their cars in the top ten. But Rome was brutally bumpy, and we knew the driveshaft was our weak link. We'd already seen it fail during practice in Santiago, another circuit where the cars had to fight the bumps – but Rome was harsher still. The drive-shaft is a critical piece: a rotating shaft that delivers energy from the powertrain to the wheels.

One by one, the failures started. First Edo's car. Then Felipe's. Then one of the customer cars. Three out of four Venturi-powered cars stopped with the same issue. It was alarming. If we weren't able to fix the issue, and quickly, our season would be ruined. But a driveshaft redesign is not something you can do easily. It's a complex component, and the lead times for manu-facturing a new one are painfully long – six months at best.

My phone rang. It was Hans Werner Aufrecht – the 'A' in 'Mercedes-AMG', a legendary engineer with an equally legendary temper. His team, HWA, was preparing to run the Mercedes-Benz entry the following year. They had just announced their intention to build their own powertrain and compete. By then, Mercedes had confirmed its entry into Formula E, joining a wave of major manufacturers – Porsche, Audi, BMW and Jaguar. The championship was evolving fast, and competition was rising with it. By now, Hans Werner and his wife Roswitha were close friends of ours and had come to our wedding. I had heard all the stories of his epic outbursts but hadn't been on the receiving end of one. Until now.

He screamed down the line in German. *Das ist einfach inakzeptabel! Mach was! [It's simply unacceptable! Do something!]*

What could I say? I wasn't an engineer. I hadn't designed the driveshaft. All I could do was take the hit, wait for the rant to be over, then tell him I understood, tell him I found it just as unacceptable as he did. But inside, I felt completely dejected. Not being part of the technical team, I had no idea *how* to fix the driveshaft.

The reality hit hard. This wasn't a one-off issue. It was a problem that would haunt us all season if we couldn't find a fix. And at that moment, I didn't see a way out.

Then Toto called.

Have you spoken to Hans Werner?

Yes.

He's really, really not happy.

I know, Toto, but what do you want me to do? I don't know how to design a new driveshaft. That's not on my shoulders.

Silence. Then, in his usual, matter-of-fact way, he said, *You are the Team Principal, Susie. It's your problem to fix.*

I felt the rage bubble up. On the one hand, Toto had always been my greatest supporter – he believed in me, always fought my corner. But in moments like this, when the pressure was suffocating, he had a way of cutting through everything with brutal honesty. And this time, it stung.

I slammed the phone down, fuming. Then a text message came through. It was from Toto. A contact: the CEO of Pankl, our driveshaft manufacturer.

I called immediately.

It was Sunday afternoon but he picked up and was completely understanding of the issue and urgency.

Let us look into it and then all meet on Tuesday to see if we can find a solution. I can't guarantee anything.

From the race ending on Sunday to that meeting on Tuesday morning, I buried myself in everything I could learn about driveshafts. By 9 a.m., my Technical Director and I were sitting in a room with a sea of Pankl engineers, fighting to salvage our season.

A completely new driveshaft design wasn't possible in the timeframe but six weeks later, after a monumental effort from both sides, we had an updated reinforced driveshaft in the car. Not only did the driveshaft hold, but Felipe finished on the podium in Monaco, in front of Gildo and our home crowd.

I spent those six weeks applying maximum pressure – demanding daily, even hourly updates to keep the urgency high and the momentum constant. It was a hard-earned lesson: when the going gets tough, the tough get going. When people tell you something is impossible, when every solution seems out of reach, sometimes, it just comes down to refusing to give up.

That season, while promising, made one thing clear – we still had a long way to go to consistently fight for race wins and, ultimately, the championship. Our powertrain, the heart of an electric car, was quick but lacked the energy efficiency of our competitors. As a result, we had to conserve power, losing speed as the races wore on.

One of the biggest challenges was negotiating a new powertrain deal for the following season while still being locked into our current contract. As a customer team, we didn't build our own powertrain – but we could choose our powertrain supplier. Given Mercedes' dominance in Formula One, backing their new powertrain felt like a safe bet. Following months of discussions and exit negotiations, we made a big step forward – Venturi would switch to the Mercedes-Benz powertrain. We had enabled their entry into Formula E by granting them access to our exclusive power-train supplier during their preparation season, and now they would be supplying us.

After our race in Monaco, it was the Monaco F1 Grand Prix. I had come over with Jack, planning to spend a few days in the office while Toto focused on his race weekend. One evening, I rushed back from work, spent time with Jack, got him ready for bed, and then hurried to get myself ready for dinner. Toto arrived back from the track, took one look at me and said flippantly, *You look exhausted.*

I exploded.

I look exhausted? I am *exhausted!*

Everything poured out – the relentless effort to turn the team around, the constant travel, the pressure to be a good mother, a good wife. I told him I felt like I was drowning under it all.

He held his hands up, then came over and embraced me in a hug. *Okay, okay. Let's sit down and talk about this properly after dinner.*

To his credit, he listened. He knew I carried the weight of managing Jack, especially with his Formula One schedule keeping him on the road. But this time, he didn't just acknowledge it – he asked what he could do to make it easier.

We worked out a plan. I would spend more time in Monaco. That way, I could be in the office more, reducing the constant back-and-forth travel. Toto would come to Monaco whenever he had free time, so I didn't always feel the pressure to get back home. It was a small shift, but it made a huge difference.

By the end of the season, we had finished eighth in the championship – still midfield, but finally seen as a team on the rise. The biggest challenge now, however, was not technical. It was financial. With no sponsors on the car, our commercial prospects were stark. The balance sheet looked bleak, and I knew that I needed to turn my focus to making the team financially sustainable.

Sponsorship in Formula E was difficult. The series was gaining traction and was seen as an exciting new frontier, but convincing brands to invest was another story. We didn't yet have the level of exposure in place, no global broadcast deals and no established fanbase. So I sat down and did my research, spending months approaching brands that could fit our narrative. Then I decided to focus on all the brands I could already see in motorsport. Who understood the industry and might see Formula E as a new opportunity? That was when I came across a new title partner of a Formula One team. I mentioned it to Liz, telling her it was a company I wanted to approach. She immediately said, *Oh, I know the guy who brokered that deal. I can put you in touch.*

And so I was introduced to Chris Welch. We met in New York, where I told him about my vision for the team and how I'd love to bring a new title partner into Venturi. That conversation led to a meeting at Farnborough airport in Hampshire. Gildo, myself, Chris and the founder of the company sat down, and I presented the opportunity for them to become our title partner.

The sticking point? The colour of the car. Their title partnership in F1 was causing discontent because the team wouldn't change the colour of the car. Well, that was an easy one for us to solve.

Join us and you can paint our car whatever colour you want.

He signed as our new title sponsor. It was a breakthrough moment, and yes, the car changed colour, but that first sponsor helped us to secure three additional new partners, and from there, the building blocks fell into place.

These new sponsorship deals put us on a secure footing and meant we turned up with a whole new look for the following season. Gone was the blue and silver, replaced with red, black and white. The car design, driver suits and team kit were all new. Outside of that, Formula E was gaining serious momentum. The media had even begun speculating whether it could challenge Formula One. That sort of coverage was exciting, but I saw them as entirely different entities. Formula One had the weight of history behind it, the fastest cars in the world and a deeply ingrained global presence. Formula E, on the other hand, was the ambitious disruptor, pioneering electric technology and bringing racing directly to city centres instead of expecting fans to travel to circuits. It was a fresh concept, but not a direct competitor to F1: they could exist together.

The season began with promise. Once again, the opening race took place in Saudi Arabia, on a street circuit in Riyadh – a tight, technical track carved through a UNESCO World Heritage site. The year before had been an historic moment, as Saudi Arabia hosted Formula E as the country's first-ever international sporting event. In an unprecedented move, visas were granted to anyone with a race ticket. It was a bold move by Alejandro and the Formula E leadership, yet there was hesitancy, particularly among the women in the paddock.

I was approached to serve as an ambassador for the race. My immediate reaction? Absolutely not. Women had only just been granted the right to drive. I still remember a conversation from two years earlier at the Bahrain Grand Prix when I was with Williams. A journalist had asked me how it felt to be an F1 test driver when, just 25 kilometres away across the causeway, women in Saudi Arabia weren't allowed behind the wheel. It was a stark reminder of the cultural divide.

Then came an invitation to a meeting where Formula E and representatives from the Saudi government laid out their vision. The country was undergoing massive transformation under the new Crown Prince, with an ambition to open up in ways previously unimaginable. Their message was clear: change was coming. I could either support and be part of that change or sit on the sidelines and criticise. I wanted to support it, but first, I needed to see it for myself.

A few weeks later, I travelled to Saudi Arabia with the Formula E management team, cautious but open-minded. As I stepped off the plane, I instinctively pulled a scarf over my head and wore a long-sleeved, high-necked jumper, unsure of what to expect. But my reservations quickly eased. Throughout my two-day visit, I dressed in my usual team attire, attended lunches and dinners alongside an all-male group, and never once felt out of place. I left with a genuine sense of optimism – change wasn't happening overnight, but it was real and deliberate.

That experience stayed with me. Years later, when I took over F1 Academy and pushed to race alongside Formula One, Saudi Arabia was the first promoter to step forward and offer us a support race slot. Their actions had always spoken louder than their words.

At the following race in Marrakech, murmurs began in the paddock about the next race in China possibly being cancelled due to a virus outbreak. At first, it seemed like just another logistical hurdle, but then the race was officially cancelled, and soon after, the entire world came to a halt. The Covid-19 pandemic had arrived, and motorsport, like everything else, stopped. That posed a significant challenge. Our sponsors had invested with the expectation of a full season of racing, yet our contracts didn't account for a pandemic halting competition. I spoke with each of our partners, approaching the discussions with a willingness to compromise. To me, a true partnership meant navigating both the highs and lows together.

But we were in uncharted territory. While Formula One swiftly adapted, creating controlled bubbles at permanent circuits, Formula E faced far greater challenges – our entire series depended on street racing in city centres. With strict lockdowns in place and no cure on the horizon, there was no clear timeline for our return. Uncertainty loomed, not just over our team's survival but over the future of the championship itself.

For the first time, Toto and I were forced to step off the relentless treadmill of motorsport. We had uninterrupted months together with Jack – no flights, no races, no constant movement. It was a rare pause. Although I had the stress of managing the uncertainty and when we would go back racing, it was all much easier without the constant movement and pressure to perform on the track. My focus was on what I could control, ensuring the team survived.

For Toto, though, this stillness didn't come easily. He thrived on momentum – races, negotiations and constant decision-making. Without it, a restlessness settled in, an unease that he struggled to shake. He admitted to feeling disconnected and anxious. He had always been candid about his struggles with mental health, but lockdown stripped away the distractions that had kept them at bay. I saw the change in him. He wasn't looking for sympathy – he never did.

I don't want pity, he told me. *I just need to fix it.*

Therapy had always been part of his life, but during those months, it became an anchor. At home, we settled into our own rhythm. I instinctively kept things steady, ensuring he had the space to process what he needed to, without ever having to ask for it. But even in his own struggles, he saw an opportunity to shift the conversation around mental health.

People need to know it's okay to struggle, even the strongest do, he told me. *If I can talk about it, maybe it will contribute to breaking the stigma that mental health is a weakness. I feel the opposite of weak, but still struggle. If channelled in the right way, the sensitivity that you have can be a superpower.*

His vulnerability and the bravery it took to express it had an unexpected effect on the sport. It also encouraged openness within Mercedes, pushing for a culture where acknowledging stress wasn't a weakness but a sign of strength. For me, it wasn't just about supporting him; it was about stepping up. He'd stepped in in such a big way to cut down on my travel and care for Jack, I wanted to do the same for him. I instinctively took control, ensuring stability and the essentials that kept our world turning. He needed to recalibrate, and that meant I had to be the one holding it together so he could find his footing again. What he was doing was important, showing men that it was okay, even healthy, to express feelings.

Despite its hardships, that period reaffirmed something I already knew: no matter how much I thrived on challenge and ambition, our family came first. But it also brought the age-old question into sharper focus: can women truly have it all? For me, the answer was simple. I wanted both – a fulfilling career and a strong family life. But not at any cost. Ambition would never come at the expense of my family. The better that Toto and I could express our vulnerabilities and support each other at home, the better we could help each other thrive at work.

Through all of lockdown, we leaned on what we had always understood about each other: we knew what it meant to fight for our place in the world. Toto often called it a 'warrior approach' – a mindset shaped by the battles we'd each faced, even if they came from different places. His were financial hardships and personal loss: his father being diagnosed with brain cancer, losing the family wealth in his decline and eventually passing away when Toto was just fourteen. Mine were years of proving myself in an environment that wasn't built for me.

Toto never hid from the difficulties of his past. He credited them with forging his resilience, and he saw that same grit in me. We spoke often about adversity – not in a performative way, but as a quiet, mutual recognition. For him, those early struggles became the source of his ambition. Everything difficult I experienced as a child became my motivation. It taught me how to keep pushing when others might give up.

He understood instinctively that my path had been shaped by navigating a male-dominated sport, where I was often the outsider. We both learned that nobody hands you anything. You fight for it. You persist. You endure. You never back down. For Toto, adversity wasn't just something to survive – it was fuel. I understood that deeply. I'd done the same on and now off the track. It was why, when lockdown finally lifted, we were ready to go.

When Formula E finally announced its return, the plan was intense – six races over nine days in Berlin so that a set number of races had been completed and the season could be deemed concluded. It would be brutal, but we had a real shot at finishing sixth in the championship. Edo was proving to be a front-runner, but there was another major issue looming – our driver lineup.

Felipe Massa had been a huge signing for the team. A former Ferrari Formula One driver, he brought commercial value, credibility and experience. But he also came with a high salary – one that wasn't sustainable for a smaller team like ours. And with our finances hit so hard because of the lockdown, the difficult task of finding an exit strategy for Felipe fell to me.

I had known Felipe for years and had enormous respect for

him, both as a driver and as a person. Ending his contract mid-season, during the intense Berlin races, was far from ideal but was contractually the only exit clause we had. But I approached him directly, telling him I felt our journey together was coming to an end. More importantly, I wanted the decision to be his. He'd only scored three points all season. Some of that was on us as a team, but it was still nowhere near where either of us had hoped to be. We handled it professionally, and at the end of those six races, we released a statement confirming that Felipe would be leaving at the end of the season.

It wasn't an easy situation, but it was necessary. The team was evolving, and we had to make tough choices to secure our future. Tougher still was the outcome of the Berlin races. What could have been a solid sixth in the championship crumbled, we lacked pace in qualifying so both drivers would be starting midfield. Edo scored just a handful of points after some tough wheel-to-wheel racing and Felipe none – we ended up ninth.

I was livid, and the subsequent disappointment lingered for weeks. I put the final championship standings on a giant poster in the office – a constant reminder of the sting, fuelling our motivation. We were better than ninth. Despite all our progress, the standings just didn't reflect our capabilities. But I also couldn't ignore the positives – even with all the difficulties of the season, we had shown real promise. Heading into the next one, I believed we were finally ready to mount a serious title challenge.

However, as if I didn't have enough going on during that season, Gildo told me he felt it was time to sell. We were financially and competitively, as a team, in a strong position and he had his sights set on a new project – building an electric rover to go to Mars. He was ready to move on. I wasn't. I felt like I had unfinished business. I had joined to turn this team around, and we weren't there yet. I wanted to win.

But our agreement had always been clear – if one of us wanted to exit, the other would follow. We were aligned in everything, including the exit strategy. And so, I was tasked with selling the team. My first call was to Alejandro Agag. Confidentially, I told him we were looking to exit. Formula E was gaining traction, and interest in the series was high, but Gildo and I were both aligned on the fact it couldn't just be sold to anyone – we had to leave it in strong hands, we owed that to all of the team members. He immediately mentioned an American investor who was eager to get involved. Talks began. They were long, exhausting, and at times frustrating.

But I knew I could never let negotiations distract me from the real priority – performance on track. The stronger we were as a team, the better our chances of securing a successful sale. And if this was going to be the end of my time in Formula E, I was determined to go out on a high.

The following season was a breakthrough. We'd fought so hard to get there – through setbacks, sacrifices, the pressure of expectation – and now, at last, it felt like something was shifting. The team was starting to become what I had always believed it could be. That weight I'd carried – the constant push to prove, to justify, to deliver – began to lift. And yet, in a high-performance world, there's rarely space to stop and take it in. One result rolls into the next, and your focus shifts almost instantly – what's the next race, the next gain, the next challenge? I barely paused to notice what we'd achieved. The more success we had, the more the bar moved. It's only now, looking back, that I realise how special that time was. Because in the moment, you're just holding on, giving everything, racing towards what's next.

With two wins and four podiums, we had become a team that expected to win. And the more you win, the easier it gets. You learn how to win, how to hold your nerve in those critical moments. We had that confidence, that easiness about us. Edo had come within seven points of becoming Formula E World Champion, and our performance that season allowed us to secure a championship-winning driver for the following year. Suddenly, we were heading into the new season as title contenders.

Though Toto oversaw Mercedes' Formula E entry, his F1 commitments kept him away from most races. But when he did attend, Alejandro had a little fun with the broadcast graphics. Instead of the usual *Head of Mercedes-Benz Motorsport*, the screen simply read: *Susie's husband*. Toto took it in good humour. He wanted success for Mercedes – but, naturally, he wanted it for me too.

With everything in place – two top-tier drivers, a competitive car, strong sponsorship and the team sale finalised – the venture was both a sporting and financial success. In what would be my final season in Formula E, I stepped up to be CEO. The sleepless nights, the relentless fight to secure the best talent, restructure operations and attract sponsors felt like a distant battle. Now, the team was streamlined, efficient and undeniably competitive – a feat that didn't go unnoticed. We were a customer team running on a fraction of the budget of some of our competitors, but we had built a team capable of fighting at the very front, with two cars ready to challenge for the championship.

In my last season at the helm, we were the team to beat. Five wins – more than any other team. Both drivers in the podium fight, race after race. We fell just twenty-four points short of the team championship, edged out by Mercedes. From where I had started to where I finished, it was a success story in every sense and it felt time for me to set my sights on a new challenge.

I had enjoyed working with Gildo. He had given me full authority at Venturi, trusted me completely, and given me the chance to prove what I was capable of. Now, he wanted to do it again. He asked if I'd come and run his new space project.

Let's do it just like before. Same deal, same terms.

15

BEFORE I could fully commit to what came next, Formula One delivered a reminder of just how brutal and unpredictable the sport could be. The 2021 Abu Dhabi Grand Prix was meant to be a celebration – the culmination of one of the most intense seasons in Formula One history. Both Max Verstappen and Lewis Hamilton were deserving champions but this wasn't just another race. It was a battle that would define a legacy and, I hoped, would cement Lewis as the greatest Formula One driver of all time with his eighth world title.

I watched in the background as the tension built with every lap. Lewis was faultless, in complete control, and it looked as though he had done everything right to secure an eighth world title. But then, with just five laps to go, everything changed. A late-race crash brought out the safety car, bunching up the field. In normal circumstances, either all lapped cars would be allowed through, or none at all. Instead, in a move that defied all precedent and protocol, the race director took a single decision that wasn't in the regulations and that the sport had never seen before: following a crash, he allowed just the cars between Lewis and Max to unlap themselves behind the safety car. As the regulations stated, you either allow all the cars to unlap themselves, or none. This handed the victory to Max.

In the Mercedes garage, disbelief gave way to anger. Toto, usually so measured, was on the radio demanding explanations. None of the responses he was offered made sense. It was a moment that shook his belief in the sport's governance. *The stopwatch never lies*, he always said. But in that moment, human error had dictated the outcome and in the wider paddock, many were deeply unsettled and critical, feeling the situation had been mishandled and had compromised the integrity of the sport.

In the days that followed, I had a deep feeling of injustice. This wasn't about losing – it was about how it happened. I decided to speak publicly, posting on Instagram to express my thoughts – not just as Toto's wife or as someone inside the sport but as someone who believed in fairness. This wasn't about diminishing Max's achievement; both were deserving champions. It was about the fundamental principles that had always defined racing – clarity, integrity, consistency. And in this instance, it felt like Lewis had been cheated of a record-breaking eighth World Championship title.

Privately, Toto and I wrestled with it. The team had still managed to win their eighth constructors' title, but the manner in which Lewis was robbed left us not just frustrated, but genuinely questioning the foundations of the sport. It took weeks for the disappointment and hollow feeling to lift, not helped by the fact that everywhere we went, people couldn't help but comment on what had happened in Abu Dhabi. It came up in every conversation, every dinner, every meeting. The sense of injustice clung to us, and at times it felt like we simply couldn't escape it. We talked about it at home, at work, around the dinner table, replaying it over and over, each time hoping it might make more sense. But it didn't. For months, it was the only story.

The governing body of motorsport, the FIA (Fédération Internationale de l'Automobile), later admitted human error in how the rules were applied, and the race director was removed from his role. The safety car and race management regulations were also rewritten to prevent a repeat. Eventually, we had to draw a line under it – the next season was coming.

Soon, F1 was about to be launched into a global spotlight. Unbeknownst to us at the time, the release of a Netflix docuseries, combined with the controversy of Abu Dhabi, would propel F1's global popularity to unprecedented heights. Suddenly, my husband was being recognised everywhere we went.

With the new global attention for our sport, the business of F1 was changing dramatically. For years, the model had been built on legacy power struggles, where the strongest teams dominated and financial inequality meant that only a handful of teams could realistically fight for wins. That's just how it was. Nobody questioned it – until Liberty Media took over, bringing an American sports model to a sport that traditionally had been resistant to outside influence.

Toto and I often discussed in the early days how different the mindset was in the US compared to Europe. The way American sports are structured is different: they balance competitiveness through measures like salary caps and draft systems to ensure long-term sustainability. That mindset was about making the whole league successful, not just a handful of dominant teams. Formula One had never worked like that. It had always been about spending power – the more you spend, the faster you go – and the biggest teams fought (and spent) ruthlessly to protect their advantage. Toto admitted that even he had been sceptical about the American influence on the sport. When Liberty Media proposed a cost cap to level the playing field, he saw it as a direct threat to Mercedes' dominance. He didn't like it at the beginning because Mercedes had the financial firepower and had already built a winning machine, and suddenly, they were being told to limit their spending and narrow the gap between them and the smaller teams. But over time, he recognised that this shift was necessary for the long-term health of the sport.

One other interesting point Toto made was how the new sporting regulations functioned like a draft system in the NFL. In American sports, the weakest teams were given the first pick of the best new players, ensuring that no single team could dominate forever.

Formula One's version of this was to allocate more wind tunnel time to smaller teams, allowing them to conduct extra aerodynamic tests. Crucially, this gave smaller teams a better chance of improving their performance, helping to close the gap to the front. Spending across the board was capped. Efficiency became everything. The era of outspending your rivals was over.

I saw how difficult this change was for Toto, even though he could see the overall benefits to the sport. On the one hand, he wanted Mercedes to win every race, every season. But on the other, he recognised that if the sport itself wasn't healthy, none of that would matter. What was the point of winning in a series that had become predictable, where fans lost interest because only two or three teams had any real chance of success?

This became especially clear during the pandemic, when Formula One, like every other sport, was shaken to its core. The 2020 season opener in Melbourne was cancelled just hours before the first practice session. By July, racing resumed under strict health protocols and team bubbles, but every event was held behind closed doors. With no crowds, race-day revenue and sponsor exposure dropped dramatically, hitting the sport's finances hard. Financial sustainability became a bigger issue than ever, and suddenly, the cost cap wasn't just an idea – it was a necessity. Teams that had once resisted it now realised they wouldn't survive without it. That was the turning point. It wasn't about restricting competition, it was about ensuring there was still a competition to fight for.

As much as some purists resisted the American influence, there was no denying that the sport was growing because of it both in terms of audience reach and cultural relevance. It became a catalyst for a younger and more diverse fanbase.

New markets were opening up, young drivers were getting more opportunities, and crucially, smaller teams could now dream of success rather than just survival. I'd been in the paddock long enough to see how many teams had collapsed under financial pressure, how many great names had disappeared because they simply couldn't keep up with the spending war. That was never going to be sustainable.

Toto said, *I don't care what Wikipedia says about our race wins or Mercedes' titles. What matters is meeting my own expectations, sustaining long-term success for the team. But no team operates in isolation – long-term competitiveness isn't just about winning today, it's also about ensuring the sport remains strong for the future. Every team has a responsibility to keep the competition fierce, the innovation relentless, and the spectacle alive, because the health of Formula One depends on all of us.*

Winning meant nothing if the foundations of the sport weren't strong. Formula One had been transformed and Liberty Media's influence, with new US races in Miami and Las Vegas coupled with stronger commercial deals, had turned it into a global entertainment powerhouse. *Drive to Survive*, the hugely successful Netflix series, became a gateway for millions of new fans. It took F1 from a niche, technical sport into the mainstream. By humanising the drivers and lifting the curtain on the drama behind the scenes, it reached audiences who'd never watched a race before, particularly women.

I had been at circuits where the grandstands were half-empty, with only the die-hard fans showing up. Now, races were selling out months in advance. A new generation, many discovering F1 for the first time, were engaging with the sport in ways we'd never seen before, fuelled by a surge in digital and social media.

I remember arriving in Miami for the inaugural race in 2022 and walking through the airport with Toto. Suddenly, people were shouting his name, pointing, taking photos. We turned to each other, bemused. This became the new normal. Wherever we travelled to a race, people were recognising us, especially Toto, as if he were a celebrity. Young fans, many of them women, would stop us in the street or airport. Some would shout out, *I love your husband!* I'd smile and reply, *Thank you – so do I!*

There were still challenges, of course.

Not everyone agreed with the direction Formula One was taking, and some old-school voices still pushed back against the growing emphasis on entertainment. But watching from the inside, I could see the transformation and it wasn't just about showbiz and spectacle. It was about creating a business model that could support real, long-term competition. The Formula One I had entered as a driver was a different world from the one I watched now.

In 2023, the natural next step for me would have been a move into Formula One, but I wasn't interested in exploring this option. I felt that was Toto's domain, and I'd become set on finding a new challenge. Working with Gildo in the space industry intrigued me. I was keen to try something beyond motorsport. Before that, I needed to rest.

After such an intense period of being in a high-performance-focused environment with the constant pressure to deliver, I promised myself three months off – time to be with Toto and Jack, to enjoy life, and be at home. But something else was starting to stir and it was happening within my home. Quietly at first, almost imperceptible, but unmistakably there. Jack, our next generation, was beginning to show a real interest in motorsport. Not the kind you casually pick up from being around it, but something deeper, more instinctive. Something I recognised all too well.

Jack and I had always followed the races together on television when Toto was away. It was part of our fabric, background noise in our house, the rhythm of our weekends. With two parents so steeped in the sport, I suppose it was inevitable. But this wasn't just imitation. I started to notice traits in Jack that felt startlingly familiar. I could see a curiosity, a thrill, a discipline – the insistence on doing things right.

There was one Family Day in particular, organised by the Mercedes team ahead of the British Grand Prix. Jack was just over two years old. They'd taken over the grounds at Stowe near Silverstone, with lots of activities for children and a big screen to watch the race on. I was chatting with some of the other mums, and I had Jack in my sights just near the edge of the bouncy castle. Then one of them said, *And where's Jack?*

I pointed. *He's by the bouncy castle.* She looked over and laughed. *Ah, yes. I know exactly which one is yours.*

There he was – not bouncing, not launching himself into the air like the others. While all the other children threw their shoes in a heap, he was standing neatly to the side, meticulously placing every single one into a perfect line. Pair by pair. Positioned just so. He liked everything in its place – no question where he got that from.

On our visits back to Scotland, he adored getting on the little motorbikes. He'd push himself in every sport he tried. It wasn't about being the best – at least not yet – it was about effort. And as a parent, I found myself wanting for him exactly what I had in my own childhood. Not glory. Not trophies. But purpose.

I have no ambition for him to chase a career in motorsport. I want him to pursue his dreams, and if that's motorsport, great. If not, he'll find his way. What I do want him to learn are the lessons I learned from the sport: what it means to win – and perhaps more importantly, what it feels like to lose. The elation, the sting, the bounce back. The strength you build in those moments when you have to dig deep, when no one is clapping and it's just you deciding to try again. Looking at Jack as his fascination with motorsport built, I was reminded of Little Susie and the tenacity she had.

You get bombarded with parenting advice these days. But I listened to one professor speak, Russell Barkley, and his view resonated with me: as parents, we are not engineers who can design a child. Our children come to us already full of their own wiring, their own code, a genetic mosaic of extended family. Our role is that of the shepherd, to guide them to the right pastures where they can develop and grow, to nourish them and protect them from harm, to give them space to become who they already are. Now we find ourselves back at kart tracks, driven by Jack's own passion for the sport.

Toto and I sometimes talk about how different the landscape of youth sport is now compared to when we were kids. Everything's more professionalised. More structured. More intense. There's this constant noise about performance and progress and what age kids should start specialising. But we've both agreed: joy has to come first. If it's not fun – if it's not lighting him up – what's the point? Similarly, I realised that my joy came from fulfilling my own purpose. Being the best possible wife and mother was a huge part of my purpose and direction . . . but so was business.

My time off lasted just six weeks. I called Gildo.

Start sending everything over. I want to dive in.

I was enthralled. The technology, the engineering, the ambition – it was cutting edge, a steep learning curve that would push me far beyond my comfort zone. But there was a massive problem. Every major development, every key player in the space industry, was based in California. That was where our startup would need to be.

It gave me pause. My brother had been living in LA for the past couple of years, working as a commercials director and transitioning into film – so I had a reference point. I knew the pace of life there, the opportunities, but also the distance. Jack was about to start school. LA wasn't a quick hop like Monaco – it was a twelve-hour flight, a completely different time zone. The more I thought about it, the more uneasy I became. When I commit to something, I give it everything. But I knew I wasn't willing to be away from Toto and Jack that often.

It was during those weeks of uncertainty that I got a call

from Stefano Domenicali, the CEO of Formula One, and Greg Maffei from Liberty Media, who owned the sport. *What do you think about Formula One launching its own series to give young female drivers a real chance?* they asked.

The concept wasn't new – W Series had tried and ultimately failed just a few years earlier. I had been asked to get involved at the time, but while I loved the mission, I didn't have confidence in their business model, which relied heavily on external investment and sponsorship. Women's sport was gaining momentum, but making it commercially viable was still a challenge, due to the lack of interest and audience. But Formula One launching its own championship? That was different. They had the resources to invest – and the platform to build something up.

I told Stefano I thought it was a fantastic idea. *If you need any support from me on the sidelines, just let me know. It could have a huge impact.*

But he cut in. *No. You're going to run this for us.*

I hesitated. I was already deep into my next project with Gildo and felt a strong sense of loyalty to him. But of course, I had my hesitancies about having to spend so much time in Los Angeles, a world away from my family. So I flew to New York to meet with Liberty Media. They were serious – ready to invest at a level I had never imagined for women in motorsport, recognising their growing female fanbase and how male-dominated the sport was still perceived. Female participation in racing had never surpassed 5 per cent and that was down to a lack of female role models but also the high financial barrier young female drivers faced trying to progress in the sport. That was why I started Dare to be Different – because without action, nothing would change. This was a once-in-a-lifetime chance to build something that could reshape the sport. But I was torn.

After long discussions with Toto, he gave me his view.

Trust your gut instinct. But if you don't run F1 Academy, I'm not sure who should. You've been a racing driver for over twenty-five years, you have the experience at every level in the sport. You've run a team. You understand this industry inside out. And this is your chance to make a real difference.

Over the years, I'd spoken a lot about diversity in the sport but I was done talking. I felt I'd done all I could from the sidelines. Now I was being handed an opportunity that, if done right, could create real, lasting change. And deep down, I knew if I didn't take it, I'd regret it.

In March 2023, at the opening F1 race in Bahrain, I walked into the Formula One paddock – not as a driver, not as a Team Principal, but as Managing Director of F1 Academy.

A new chapter had begun.

16

N Bahrain, I met with every Team Principal and delivered the same message: *Please don't see me as a woman leading a women's initiative – this is for the greater good of our sport.* Their support was unanimous, but it came with a warning shot: we're behind you, but you have one chance to get this right. There had been many initiatives over the years, and a championship for women had been started some years before but failed in a sea of debt. There was a clear lack of interest and support from sponsors and broadcasters, leaving media coverage and visibility at low levels. It was a vicious cycle that needed to be broken. The stakes were clear – F1 Academy had to be a success.

By the time I joined, the series was already in motion, led by Bruno Michel, a highly experienced figure who had built Formula Two and Formula Three, the junior stepping stones to Formula One, into thriving championships. F1 Academy was one level lower, running Formula Four cars, the first entry point from karting, and drivers from the age of sixteen to twenty-four would be eligible.

Most junior series had a steady influx of talent and drivers would be expected to fully fund their racing, with so many competing there was always a queue of drivers with backing fighting for the top teams. In F1 this then switched to drivers being paid to race, those in the top teams earning huge salaries and bonuses linked to performance. But F1 Academy was a different challenge. The reality was stark – there simply weren't enough young women racing, there was a clear lack of funding and there was a real danger of running out of female talent if we didn't also increase participation. With only fifteen cars on the grid, five junior teams running three drivers each, and a financial model that split costs between drivers, teams and F1 Academy, the assumption was that sponsorship would cover the gaps.

When I attended my first F1 Academy race after Bahrain, it was a shock. I had never seen such an empty race track. Aside from the teams and drivers there were no spectators. Without visibility and exposure, how would F1 Academy sustain the investment necessary to succeed? The teams were basically bleeding money. That also impacted the drivers themselves – they were struggling to even afford travel, let alone find the budget to contribute to their racing expenses. I had navigated the same struggle and knew how tough it was. Growing a fanbase was critical. Without it, our business model couldn't be viable.

If this was going to work, we had to build a solid foundation from the start – one that wouldn't just fill a quota but actually increase participation and unearth the most talented young women in motorsport, giving them a real shot at success. This wasn't just about diversity – it was about performance, and securing the financial support for that performance. If we did this right, it would create a real pathway, one that could lead the very best to the top of the sport.

In my view, there were two key reasons why the sport hadn't attracted more women. First, there was no clear role model – sometimes, you have to see it to believe it. Since I had stepped away from F1, there had been no one to inspire the next generation. That led to the second problem: participation. The numbers simply didn't work. If there weren't enough women competing, the best couldn't rise to the top. The same applied to off-track roles. By then, there were many successful women in the paddock, but they weren't in visible, high-profile positions. If we didn't showcase them, we couldn't use them to inspire the next wave.

I told Stefano I needed time to figure out the right way forward. I dived into research, reaching out to people in the sport whose opinions I trusted – those who had been around long enough to see what worked and what didn't. I asked them to be brutally honest. What needed to be done to make F1 Academy a success? How could we get more young women into motorsport?

One of my first calls was to Hugh Chambers, CEO of Motorsport UK. They held all the data – how many young women were entering karting, how many progressed to higher levels, and what initiatives had already been tried. Our discussions led me to karting races, where Hugh introduced me to James Geidel, the promoter of the European and World Karting Championships.

Walking through those paddocks was like stepping back in

time. I met so many familiar faces from my karting days – people who had once seemed like gods to me. One of them was Dino Chiesa, the man who had run Lewis Hamilton and Nico Rosberg in their junior years. Suddenly, I wasn't just a young driver in awe – I was sitting at the table with the major karting manufacturers, asking the crucial questions: *Why aren't we seeing more girls in racing? What can we do about it?*

The consensus was clear: we needed to start earlier. In motorsport, most professional drivers begin karting by the age of eight. But when you looked around the entry lists at the grassroots level, the number of young girls competing was painfully small. There simply wasn't the visibility. Motorsport didn't feel like an obvious choice for them – not in the way it so often does for boys.

If a little boy has a birthday party, it's not unusual for it to involve cars, go-karting or some form of racing. For girls, it's very rare. There was a lack of connection, of access. The sport hadn't been presented to them as something they could belong to. And all of it traces back to the same issue: role models. If you can't see it, it's harder to believe you can be it. For too long, motorsport had been a male-dominated space, not just in its paddocks but in its cultural imagination. But it was shifting. The broader momentum in women's sport, the growing female fanbase, the cultural emphasis on representation – it was all changing the landscape.

In these conversations, I could always tell when I was speaking to someone who had a daughter. It reminded me of that conversation about the pink car all those years ago. More often than not, they were the ones who truly understood why representation mattered. They wanted their girls to know this world was open to them too.

That's why it became clear to me that the F1 Academy couldn't just be about running a racing series. It had to be a parallel approach. One that looked both at the top and the bottom of the pipeline. And that's where F1 Academy Discover Your Drive was born, an overarching initiative encompassing all our efforts in karting. We supported initiatives to get more young girls into karts for the first time, established scholarships to support the most talented drivers in each category, created a driver development guide to give them the tools, insights, and guidance. At its core, it was a numbers game: the more girls we had competing, the greater the chances of the best rising to the top.

The discussions also extended beyond karting. I turned to people with deep knowledge of junior single-seater racing, like Fred Vasseur, now Ferrari's Team Principal but an old friend of Toto's and a respected figure in the sport. He had been to our wedding, and over the years, he had become a friend to me as well. He owned his own junior team, and his insight was invaluable.

During one of our conversations, he mentioned that Ferrari already had a female driver in its young driver academy. She was about to race in Formula Four so they could enter her into F1 Academy and paint the car red. I pushed him – would he put the Ferrari logo on it? He hesitated but agreed he could make it clear the driver had Ferrari's support. That planted an idea. If Ferrari would do it, why not get all ten F1 teams involved – they'd all pledged their support in Bahrain, after all. But now, what I wanted had changed. I realised I didn't just need the support of the F1 teams. I wanted to change the entire business model of F1 Academy, and I needed them to do it. I wanted to bring everything in-house, centralise the assets, secure our own commercial partners, and, most importantly, race alongside F1. Running on empty tracks with no visibility wasn't an option. F1 Academy needed the global stage of F1, where grandstands were already full and fans were engaged. *That* was how we could secure its future.

Fred thought it was a long shot but reiterated his support. I called Zak Brown at McLaren next. When I pitched the idea, he didn't hesitate. *Send me the details,* he said, *but count McLaren in.*

With Ferrari and McLaren on board within days, I went to Toto. I laid out my plan, and he immediately challenged the details. If you bring a plan to Toto, it has to be airtight – every detail considered, every obstacle anticipated. He raised an eyebrow.

You know getting all ten teams on board and signing the same legal document is close to impossible?

I know, but I'm going to try.

He nodded. *Get the others on board first, and then Mercedes will have to follow.*

It wasn't a surprise – we both understood the rules of the game and respected the boundaries.

A meeting was set up with Stefano, the CEO of F1, and his top management to present my vision. After lengthy discussions, they agreed – *Go for it.* I had the green light. Now, I just had to make it happen.

With Ferrari and McLaren already in, my next target was the other top team, Red Bull. That had the potential to be tricky. The fierce, sometimes brutal competition between Christian Horner and Toto was no secret, and I knew that could be a roadblock. But Red Bull worked with CAA, one of the biggest agencies in sports sponsorship, and I had strong allies there – Paul Danforth, Matt O'Donohoe and Judee Ann Williams. Years earlier, when I was with Williams, I'd nearly signed with them for representation and they were the best in the business, so I picked up the phone. I talked them through the idea and asked if they thought Red Bull might be interested. They saw the potential but said it wasn't their decision. They would meet with Christian to present it and, ultimately, it was up to him.

Monaco Grand Prix weekend arrived, and I had meetings lined up with multiple Team Principals. This was going to be a crucial weekend and I was on a roll. I still needed the final teams to commit, but I believed in what I was building, and that belief gave me confidence.

The first was with Christian. I don't know the exact details of what CAA said to him, but by the time I sat down, he didn't just agree to take one car for Red Bull and another for their sister team – he wanted three. That was a pivotal breakthrough.

With Red Bull, Ferrari and McLaren on board, we now had serious momentum. Next was Alpine. They had been supportive from the start and committed immediately. Then there was Günther Steiner at Haas. Back in Bahrain, he'd told me, *I'll support you in whatever way I can – just don't ask me for money.*

So when I sat down with him in Monaco, I got straight to the point, like he always was.

Günther, remember how I promised not to ask you for money?

He threw his hands up, laughing. *I knew it! I knew you'd ask eventually.*

I explained the plan, and he nodded. *Okay, sounds strong. Count us in.* I assured him that if Haas struggled to find the sponsorship, we'd sit together and find a way, but that never needed to happen. Günther delivered on his word.

By the end of the Monaco weekend, I had commitments from seven of the ten teams – enough for Mercedes to come on board as well. That gave me all the leverage I needed. The remaining teams had a choice: get on board or risk being left behind. No team wanted to be the one left sitting on the sidelines.

What had once felt like an impossible dream was now edging closer to reality. But securing all ten teams' signatures on a single legal document pledging their support to F1 Academy was no small task. We were in uncharted territory. This was the first time in the sport's 75-year history that every team was committing their name and livery to a series outside of Formula One. Every clause was picked apart by ten different sets of lawyers, and nothing about the process was straightforward. But I had F1's legal team behind me, and together, we worked around the clock – resolute in our aim to get it over the line.

In July 2023, all ten teams signed the same document. This was transformative for F1 Academy. We had achieved what many thought impossible, and it was a huge relief. I allowed myself a brief moment of pride at what we had achieved, but I didn't have time to dwell on its significance; I had to focus on getting all the other jigsaw pieces into place.

It was not an option to keep racing on empty circuits, so with the help of the F1 Race Promotion team, we began approaching race promoters to ensure F1 Academy could race alongside F1 – on the same weekend, hours before the Grand Prix. Some promoters were immediately keen, others were hesitant, and it took several months before we could piece together a viable calendar. Stefano stepped in on several occasions to push deals over the line, and in October, it was announced that F1 Academy would be a support series at seven F1 race weekends across three continents and included some of the most iconic events on the calendar: Miami, Singapore and Abu Dhabi. With the teams and the calendar locked in, my next task was clear.

I still had six liveries to fill. Having ten F1 team liveries racing alongside empty, unbranded cars wasn't an option. We needed commercial partners to step up and be part of this new era in motorsport. Their backing – and their reach – would help us grow our audience and build a strong brand identity. More people needed to know that F1 Academy existed.

American fashion designer Tommy Hilfiger was one of the first to call, saying, *Count on my support*. This wasn't just about a small logo on an F1 car – he now had an entire livery to design. Then came Puma, already well established in the paddock, signing on to back the series. But I also wanted to find a partner that would attract a new audience, a brand with a strong female focus.

A friend from my DTM days worked with beauty brand entrepreneur Charlotte Tilbury and knew her well. Her company was considering expanding into women's sport and had reached out about supporting a driver. I called immediately. *Don't just back one driver – become a partner of F1 Academy.* Within ten minutes of our first conversation, I knew we'd work together. Charlotte Tilbury's mission was a perfect fit: empowering young women, building confidence and proving they could chase their dreams. Her mantra said it all – Dare to dream it. Dare to believe it. Dare to do it.

I had never worn much makeup myself, but I didn't want these young drivers to feel they had to fit into a mould – that they had to be tomboys to be taken seriously. If one wanted to wear a full face of makeup under her helmet, that didn't make her any less of a racing driver. If another wanted to wear none at all, that was just as valid. This was about celebrating individuality, not conforming to outdated stereotypes.

The Charlotte Tilbury partnership was a breakthrough. Our announcement and the bold car livery they had designed, hot lips plastered all over a racing car, was something the sport had never seen before. It was exciting. It was *new*. I wanted to disrupt, to do things differently, and the Charlotte Tilbury team were well versed in exactly what would generate the headlines and impact. It put F1 Academy firmly on the map with a new audience outside of motorsport. It was the first time a female-founded, female-led, female-focused brand had stepped into motorsport and I knew it had had an impact when Rosi, my stepdaughter, who had never been that interested in motorsport, called from her dorm at university in the US to say she couldn't believe it. *It was so cool.*

The feedback from press and social media was huge and when Charlotte Tilbury, standing in front of her F1 Academy hot lips branded car, ended up on the front cover of the *Financial Times* 'How to Spend It' supplement, it was the icing on the cake. It turned out to be the biggest brand partnership announcement in motorsport in 2024.

To further build buzz and drive awareness, many suggested we try to wedge ourselves into *Drive to Survive*, the wildly successful F1 documentary series on Netflix. But trailing in the background like a little sister hoping to be noticed? Absolutely not. We were going to have our own spotlight.

Hello Sunshine, the production company founded by Reese Witherspoon, was ready to roll the cameras, and we were actively pitching to the major streaming platforms. Just before the 2024 season began, we closed the deal: F1 Academy was coming to Netflix.

F1 Academy would now have its own platform, telling the story of these fierce young women racing on F1 Grand Prix weekends in cars that looked like miniature F1 machines.

Those images alone would reshape perceptions, inspiring the next generation to see what was possible.

Thinking back to my days as a little girl in karting, it was incredible to see how far we'd come. This was always the hope – that people would realise motorsport is one of the few sports in the world, like sailing or horse riding, where men and women can compete side by side. F1 Academy gives female drivers the financial backing and support of the best junior teams to give them a better chance of being prepared to compete at the highest levels. No separate leagues. No adjusted benchmarks. Just one track, one start line.

The common thread between those sports? They all involve something beyond the athlete, whether it's a powerful machine or a half-tonne animal. Even though women can be just as competitive, those sports remain male-dominated spaces. That's changing. Slowly, but surely. And in many ways, their dynamics mirror the business world: progress, yes, but often still on uneven ground.

That's where Formula One holds such unique power. Its reach is global. Its audience is growing, especially among young women: 42 per cent of F1 fans are now female, with 18 to 24-year-old women forming the fastest-growing demographic. This is such a huge shift compared to when I was racing, to see that young women were now engaging and interested in the sport. The conversation has moved from 'can women compete?' to 'how do we remove the barriers that remain?' That shift alone is powerful.

But inspiration isn't enough. Progress takes more than

storytelling. It demands action. Accountability. And the willingness to do things differently. I've lived the reality of stepping into rooms where I was the only woman. I know how isolating that can feel. But I've also seen what's possible when those spaces start to shift – when they begin to reflect the diversity of the world we live in. That's when real change happens.

When women are visible in leadership, they create pathways for others. When companies prioritise inclusion, they drive innovation. And when sports embrace allyship, flexibility and empathy, everyone benefits, regardless of gender. A recent study showed that 85 per cent of women in leadership roles played sport as girls. That's not a coincidence. Sport shapes mindset. It teaches resilience. It gives you a sense of belonging – and of what it means to win and lose as part of something bigger than yourself.

The future of our industry should be shaped by potential, not outdated assumptions of who belongs where. This isn't just about sport. It's about leadership. It's about showing what's possible. And in this moment, Formula One isn't just keeping pace. It's leading.

The recent surge in women's sport hasn't happened by chance. It's part of a much wider cultural shift – one fuelled by a convergence of social, cultural and commercial forces. The momentum has been building for years, but in the past few years, it's accelerated at a pace few could have predicted. Suddenly, there's visibility. Investment. Fan engagement at record levels. Women's leagues have been around for decades, but only now are they starting to be recognised and resourced in a way that reflects their true potential.

For F1 Academy, that momentum came at exactly the right time, although we didn't have to build a fanbase from scratch or fill a stadium from the ground up – we had the platform of Formula One, one of the biggest global sports properties in the world. That gave us reach. But more than that, it gave us credibility. The backing of F1, the commitment from all ten F1 teams, and the full support of the sport's ecosystem meant we were never seen as a side project. We were part of the future and every time I had to get my elbows out and bang on doors, I was met with support from the decision-makers in the sport, still mostly men. Bringing them on the journey, making them part of the mission rather than just observers – the collective effort meant the barriers fell faster as the progress accelerated.

The comparison with the WNBA is striking. It launched twenty-eight years ago, but only in the past five years has it really seen exponential growth. By contrast, F1 Academy, backed by the full weight of the F1 infrastructure, has moved considerably faster. Of course, there are still questions, particularly around the financial sustainability of women's sport in the mid-to-long term. But the commercial indicators are strong. Arenas are selling out. Media rights deals are increasing. Franchise valuations that would've seemed unthinkable a decade ago are being reached. Brands are no longer treating women's sport as an add-on, they see it as a growth sector in its own right. And that marks a major shift.

Take Gatorade, the hydration brand owned by Pepsi. It had

been a founding partner of the WNBA twenty-eight years ago, sending a clear signal of commitment. So when Pepsi entered Formula One in 2025, their stance was just as decisive: if we're in F1, we're backing F1 Academy too. The same was true for American Express – one of their first moves? Backing F1 Academy. These brands didn't just show up, they showed intent. And that intent is what drives change. Because it's not only about supporting women's sport, it's about helping to build it.

We're seeing the beginnings of a future where parity in investment and opportunity could become the norm, not the exception, driven in part by younger, more socially conscious fans who want to see representation and inclusion in the sports they follow.

As my first year at F1 Academy came to a close and the F1 season wound down, I felt a deep sense of contentment. We had made meaningful progress in a short space of time, and working alongside the wider team had been genuinely rewarding. Our family was thriving, and I often found myself pausing, grateful for it all.

With my birthday approaching, I was in London and planned to celebrate by going to dinner and then on to the Madonna concert with some of my closest friends from Monaco who had flown over specially. As I was getting ready to leave the F1 offices in Mayfair, a member of the communications team came to find me.

We think the FIA is launching an investigation into a conflict of interest, he said. *You running F1 Academy and Toto at Mercedes.*

I scoffed.

Conflict of interest?

It was absurd. F1 Academy wasn't an FIA-governed championship. I had no contact with anyone at the FIA and I wasn't at all involved in the management of F1 – F1 Academy was a separate entity and my focus was on building it into a position of strength. I went on my way, completely unconcerned.

A leak to the media followed almost immediately, and suddenly, as I was heading to dinner, my phone blew up. The insinuation of the FIA's announcement was that there might have been improper sharing of confidential information between Toto and me. My reputation was under attack even as I worked to build something positive for the sport.

I issued a firm statement, drafted throughout dinner and the concert, but within twenty-four hours, it had spiralled – 600 articles calling my integrity into question. Stefano immediately stepped up and said F1 would be backing me fully. There were reports in the media that claimed other Team Principals had raised concerns.

Unbeknownst to me, the other ten F1 teams swiftly came together and issued a joint statement of support – publicly affirming their confidence in me and making clear they saw no conflict of interest and had made no complaint. It was entirely unexpected and unprecedented. Their united response and support moved me deeply.

Just forty-eight hours later, the FIA backed down and dropped their investigation, without having done any investigating, but the story was out there. The damage was done.

How could a governing body operate in this way? Launching an unfounded inquiry, smearing someone's name, and then quietly retracting it when challenged? It was unacceptable, and only fuelled my fury and discontent further. I would not let it stand.

After Christmas, I decided to take legal action, filing a defamation case. I wanted transparency and accountability – I needed to know who had decided this was the right course of action. My integrity had been questioned, my reputation put at risk, and I wasn't about to let it go unchallenged. The experience only strengthened my resolve to stand up and take on the fight.

17

THE curtains are slightly open, letting in the first light of the morning. From my bed, I can see the Jeddah skyline, a city shifting and stretching upward, glass towers catching the glow of the rising sun. I glance at the clock. Still early, but I like early. Silencing the alarm before it can chime, I slip out of bed without waking Toto. His days start later and stretch longer; we move on different schedules. I don't reach for my phone. I already know – messages stacking up, emails waiting, another day of racing unfolding. But for now, I let the quiet linger, savouring the brief calm before the schedule fills every hour of the day.

Our team clothing is laid out – Mercedes kit on one side, F1 Academy kit on the other. By now, our routines are established rhythms, and I know I might not see him again for the rest of the day. As I get ready to leave, I steal a glance his way. Nearly fifteen years together. Mum and Dad always said that when you find the right person, it only gets better with time – and they were right. It does. The deep love, this journey, the family we've built. Every day, I'm grateful we found each other, grateful to have met my soulmate. He believed in me – pushed me to be my best, never seeing limits in what I could achieve. He fought in my corner but never shielded me from challenges, knowing they would make me stronger. I wouldn't be here if he hadn't been there.

I step out of the hotel and into the car for the short drive to the circuit. It's staggering how much has changed here in just six years – back then, women in this country were still banned from driving. But the world has changed. The needle has shifted. Liberty and F1 recognised the surge in their female fan base, the rising momentum of women's sport. They saw the chance to lead, to create opportunities in one of the few sports that isn't inherently segregated. And now, here we are – an all-female racing series has its place on an F1 Grand Prix weekend. Progress can be relentless, always pulling you towards what's next. But sometimes, in the rush to push forward, you forget to take in just how far you've come.

As I approach the F1 Academy paddock, I see my team gathered, waiting for me. They've been here long before me, ensuring every last detail is thought of and in place – by now, they know me well. I step out of the car, taking it all in. At this moment, there's nowhere else I'd rather be. With my team. At the track.

We walk together, and I look around me – the drivers getting strapped into their cars, the garages lined with the unmistakable colours of each F1 team and our partners. These iconic brands aren't just here, they're fully backing F1 Academy.

It's such a familiar setting for me, but now something feels different.

Women are everywhere. Not just a few but a real, undeniable presence. Engineers, mechanics, team members – working, thriving. And beyond them, the fans. So many female fans. There's a confidence in them, an ease. No questioning their place. No hesitancy. They belong.

As we arrive in the F1 pit lane on our way to the starting grid, I glance into the Mercedes garage. The familiar black and silver cars sit poised, engineers milling around, deep in their work. There's an undeniable shift in the air – preparations not just for another race but for a future without Lewis Hamilton at the helm. Twelve years of Toto and Lewis. A partnership that defined an era. And now, it's coming to an end. A new chapter on the horizon with George Russell and the young rookie Kimi Antonelli.

Further down the paddock, I pass familiar faces, hands lifting in recognition. When I reach the Williams garage, I spot people I still recognise, and it doesn't surprise me. Williams has always inspired deep loyalty – the kind that keeps people anchored, even as the sport shifts around them. I think back to the days when I sat in that Williams car, the raw sensation of driving a Formula One car. A young girl's dream coming true. I proved that a woman could be fast, that there are no physical barriers keeping women from succeeding in F1. It's hard work, yes. But so is being a mother. So is running a business.

But this isn't the same team I once knew, that gave me the chance. The Williams family no longer holds the reins; private equity has taken over, steering it into the modern era. That's where F1 is now – big business. The teams that once bled money now hold immense franchise value. The game has changed.

The countdown to the race has started. As I walk onto the grid, the Netflix cameras following closely behind, I see Stefano Domenicali. We both smile. The vision has become a reality, we have created such an opportunity for young female talent, one that I could never have even dreamed of when I was a young girl.

I feel a swell of pride, of knowing that I am passing the baton. Creating a movement and not just a moment. Using everything I have learned to help the next generation avoid the mistakes I made, build on what I did right, and navigate the challenges I know all too well. I have been where they are. I know exactly how tough it was and I also know how important it is to be given the chance.

Not everyone sees it the same way. Later in the season, I'm standing in the paddock when she approaches – a name that carries weight in our sport, someone who's walked her own difficult path and had great success as a racing driver in the US. We hadn't connected before. She gets straight to the point.

Why do you care? she asks. *Why are you doing all this F1 Academy stuff?*

I pause. *Because it was hard*, I say. *And I think maybe it doesn't have to be quite so hard for the next generation.*

She doesn't hesitate. *It was tough. It is tough. They should have it tough.*

And I understand that. I understand the pride in having endured. But I also believe we can hold space for progress. I'm not here to make the road easy. I'm here to make it visible. To show what's possible. Because sometimes, all it takes is one open door to change someone's path entirely.

Look at that, Stefano says, pointing up to the grandstand where a group of young girls has gathered, watching the grid. One little girl catches my eye, standing next to her father, her small hand wrapped in his as they soak it all in. She can't be more than seven or eight, her eyes darting between the cars, the mechanics, the drivers adjusting their gloves, readying themselves for the race. The sound, the energy, the sheer scale of it all – it's overwhelming, intoxicating. I know, because I was her once.

I think back to my own childhood, my parents and brother always urging me on. *Just go for it, Susie. You've got this.* No hesitation, no doubt – just a fierce little girl who believed that she could. And I did. That was the first taste of what it meant to push past fear, to throw myself into something headfirst, trusting that if I kept going, I'd find my way.

This father, standing beside his daughter now, maybe doesn't fully realise the impact of bringing her here today. Maybe he thinks it's just a race, another weekend together. But I see how she's absorbing everything, how this moment is stirring something inside her. That flicker of possibility, the realisation that this world isn't just for the men, because if she can see it, she can believe it.

But the success of F1 Academy isn't just about seeing a woman break through to F1. It's about opening doors, breaking down barriers, and redefining what's possible in a sport that has, for too long, been seen as a man's world. It's about ensuring that the next generation not only knows opportunities exist – but understands that they have to step up, take them, and prove that they belong. Because when you show what's possible, you become the spark for the girl who never imagined she could be a racing driver – and that's how real change begins.

I take my place on the pit wall as the cars fire up. It's not the deafening roar of an F1 engine. No forty-second warm-up sequence. Just a single ignition – and then, one after another, all sixteen F1 Academy cars spring to life. They look like miniature Formula One cars as they start their warm-up lap. I see movement around me – more and more people from the garages are stepping out onto the pit wall, watching. Then, beside me appears Lewis. A seven-time world champion, possibly the greatest of all time, standing watching these young women, sending a message that their presence here matters. He understood what it meant to fight for a place in this sport. Lewis has always been more than just a driver – becoming a force for change. When the easiest path to follow is the already-trodden path, he forged his own and used his voice to challenge the status quo, pushing for greater diversity and opportunity, knowing that without action, nothing changes.

The drivers take their position on the starting grid, engines humming. The green flag is waved at the back of the grid to signal the race is ready to be started.

First light.

The girls sit motionless in their cockpits, hands tight on the wheel, eyes fixed ahead. The floodlights reflect off their visors, but underneath – steady, focused stares.

Second.

A sharper growl now, the revs climbing slightly. No more last-minute adjustments.

I look at them. Helmets on, visors down – you can't tell if these drivers are men or women. They're just racing drivers. Focused. Ready.

Third.

The noise shifts – sharper, more urgent. It's the moment when instinct will take over. No hesitation, no second-guessing. This is what they fought for. The early mornings, the endless training, the sacrifices no one saw. The times they were overlooked, doubted, dismissed. Now, none of that matters. It's just them and the track.

Fourth.

A final deep breath behind the visor. The air is electric, the engines screaming at the limit.

Fifth.

Blue smoke rises. In under a second, they'll be hurtling down the main straight – F1, and the world, watching.

A chance, an opportunity to show what they are capable of.

Now, who's going to step up and take it?

Lights out.

GO.

After six intensive months of writing, my brother and I were sitting together, talking through the book, the journey we'd been on, everything we'd poured into it. As we spoke, the conversation began to shift. He asked, 'What do you want people to take away from this? What would you say to someone younger, just starting out?' And that question stayed with me. In the following days, I kept coming back to it, and gradually, it evolved: 'What would you say to your younger self, back at the start of it all? What have you learned?' So, I began to write. What I found, as the words came out, was that it wasn't just about what I could tell her – it was about what she still had to teach me.

Dear Little Susie,

You're eight years old, and it's your first karting race. You're the only little girl on the track and you're not fast. The boys are ruthless, bumping you aside as they roar past. After your first lap, you come into the pits and tell your dad you don't like it out there.

You feel intimidated, but you're a fierce little girl, and you want to win. You have a brother who pushes you, a mother who proves that a woman can do anything, and a father who teaches you that all dreams are possible with hard work. So even though you're still scared, you go back out. You don't suddenly win; you're not even quick. But every race, you resolve to *keep* going back out, despite the knocks and the setbacks. Slowly, you start to get faster. You learn what it feels like to be a competitor. You grow stronger. You begin to challenge the boys who once pushed you aside. They hit you; you hit them back just as hard, until, finally, they respect you.

At thirteen, you glimpse a possibility and decide to dream bigger. You tell yourself you're going to make it to Formula One. It doesn't matter that there are no female racing drivers. It doesn't matter that you don't have anyone to look up to or show you the way. You are just doing what you love. This spark keeps you going when it would be easier to give up.

That choice to pursue your path, that instinct that said, *this is where I belong. This is what I want to do*. You realised you weren't going to let yourself be forced into what others expected. You weren't going to let the naysayers drown out your belief. You chose to dig deep in the moments that mattered most, to hold on to yourself. Because it takes belief – a lot of belief – to be the first in an arena where nobody looks like you.

The path was never clear, you didn't always know which road to take or which door to knock on but as you got older, you stayed fierce. Whenever a small glimpse of opportunity appeared, you seized it with both hands. The DTM test, the one-off 25 laps in a Formula One car – you were ready. You grabbed those chances with everything you had. Those little openings became pivotal moments that changed the course of your life. You knew to dig deep when the pressure was at its highest, and you managed to find something extra inside yourself to deliver. Because you always knew if you just went out and performed, the noise and doubt would fade.

But sport is brutal. There's only ever one winner, and you weren't always the one standing on top. You lost far more often than you won. The pride came from knowing you'd given every race your absolute best. Every time you picked yourself back up, dusted yourself off, and chose to come back stronger, you added another layer to your armour: a new lesson, greater resilience, sharper focus. You learned to become comfortable with the uncomfortable.

You learned to trust your gut instinct when it was time to close one chapter and start a new one. When you found your-self at a crossroads, you leaned on that instinct to make the right decision, to choose to pivot. With each new chapter, you redefined yourself and evolved, thriving on the challenge, because by then, it was what you were used to.

Sport doesn't just teach you how to win – it teaches you how to persist, how to prepare, how to understand that the real work always happens below the surface, in the moments when no one is watching. Every small moment of success – the 72 laps, the 90 minutes, the podium, the final score – is the tip of the iceberg. What lies below is the hard work, the dedication, the sacrifice. The early mornings, the late nights, the birthdays and celebrations missed. The invitations turned down because you were chasing something bigger.

As you grow older, as you become a wife and a mother, as people come to rely on you more and more, you will feel like you're no longer in the driving seat of your own destiny. The needs and wants of others will start to come before your own. It's too easy to lose sight of who you are, to drift from the fierce little girl who never saw limits. Society will always have its impressions and its ideas of what you should do or who you should be. But only you are responsible for your own happiness. Choose to be with people who lift you up and fight in your corner. Make that part of your love story. Don't get distracted by what others expect of you, or by the constant scrolling that makes you compare your journey to someone else's. Your path is your own. Stay focused on it.

There have been moments when the lows were so low that I lost sight of you, Little Susie, the girl who believed without limits. I listened to the people telling me who I should be, how I should look, what I should do. I tried to mould myself into something I was never meant to be. The expectations on a woman always seem to come from outside: you should look like this or act like that. But you didn't care what anyone thought. You loved Barbie, and you loved racing, it didn't have to be one or the other.

I realise how much harder it was than I understood at the time. Maybe that's the beauty of being a young girl: you don't realise what isn't supposed to be possible. I'm sorry I lost you sometimes, that the fierceness faded sometimes. But I always try to come back to you, the fierce, fearless little girl who saw no limits, only possibilities.

Susie

Afterword

By Toto Wolff

I⁣t was 2002 and I was racing in the FIA GT World Championship at Donington Park. Between sessions, the circuit announcer mentioned a girl competing in Formula Renault. That caught my attention. It was a fiercely competitive category, and the announcer said she'd been on the podium. That was something new – I hadn't seen any girl racing at the front in a series like that.

Lewis Hamilton was also there, and he was being talked about as the next big thing. I couldn't watch the race but the girl stuck in my mind. I hadn't even caught her surname – she was simply Susie. But the name stayed with me.

A few years later, I came to the track to assess the Mercedes DTM team that I co-owned and was introduced to all eight drivers. To my surprise, there she was. I watched Susie from a distance, talking to her engineer. She was wrapped in a thick jacket, her blonde hair was tucked back, and her cheeks were a little red from the cold.

Then I saw her get into the car. She was strapped in, visor down, transformed. Fierce. Focused. And fast. Much faster than I could ever be. Fast enough to hold her own against the best. It stopped me in my tracks.

Thank goodness she had the courage to send that text. From the first conversation, it was a coup de foudre. That moment when someone steps into your thoughts and doesn't leave. She saw me clearly, and I saw her. Our connection was instinctive. We were soulmates from the beginning.

I've watched Susie grow from a fierce racing driver into a formidable businesswoman. She is always listening, always curious. She takes everything in, decides what's worth pursuing, then dives deep if it matters to her.

It's a quality I've rarely seen; the only other person I've known like that is Lewis Hamilton. That same drive to improve, to keep learning. The mindset that says, I'm an adult, but I can still change. I can be better tomorrow than I was today.

Above all, I am so very fortunate to call her my wife. For the first time, I had met somebody I could share everything with – my thoughts, my ambitions, my insecurities – and she simply got it.

Our marriage is strong also because we are so different. She's never late and everything is timed to the second – I'm lucky if I can time myself to the hour. Her clothes are laid out the night before, in the exact order she'll put them on. Even her jewellery is lined up in sequence by the washbasin.

That's just how Susie is – disciplined, meticulous, organised to the core. And I love that about her. Truly. But after sixteen years together, it can still drive me mad. And I know the feeling is entirely mutual!

When she's on a call, she's completely locked in – nothing breaks her focus, just like when she was driving. I'll come into the room and try to distract her with funny faces behind the screen, doing everything I can to get a reaction. She doesn't flinch. Doesn't even blink. When the call ends, she looks at me, smiles, and says, 'You're such an *Arschloch*.' German for asshole. Which, coming from her, somehow always makes me laugh.

Some people still think women can't have it all – but Susie proves otherwise. She balances drive and devotion, strength and softness. There's an inner confidence that's quiet but unshakeable: in a world like Formula One, full of people trying hard to be seen, Susie stands apart. She's fiercely ambitious, relentless in her pursuit of excellence and also the most present, loving wife and mother.

Some days, as I watch her with the deepest admiration, I still catch myself wondering: how does she manage it? How can she push so hard, aim so high, and still be the anchor for our family? That's the myth she busts every day – not by trying to prove anything but by living it. By simply being Susie.

Sometimes I think she was made for me – though perhaps the truth is, we were made for each other.

Toto Wolff, Monaco, 2025

Acknowledgements

Thank you to the reader, for making it to the final page with me.

Thank you to all the people who have helped make this book. To Sarah Harvey at CAA, to my publisher Susannah Otter and to Lucy Buxton, who all brought the book to life. And to the design, sales, marketing, production and PR teams at Hodder and Stoughton.

Finally, thank you to my brilliant brother, David. I couldn't have written *Driven* without you. From our very first conversation about what this book could be, I knew I wanted you on this journey with me. You challenged me to dig deeper and revisit moments I had long buried. I'm so grateful we did this together.

Picture Acknowledgements

Pages 1, 2, above right and centre right, 4, below, and 6: Author's collection

Page 2, above left: ©1997 Chris Walker / Kartpix.net

Page 2, centre left: © Jakob Ebrey Photography

Page 2, below left: © Lyndon McNeil / Sutton Images / Getty Images

Page 2, below right: courtesy of Autosport Magazine

Page 3, above left: © 2007 Mercedes-Benz

Page 3, above right: © 2010 Mercedes-Benz

Page 3, centre left and right: © 2012 Mercedes-Benz

Page 3, below left: © 2012 Mercedes-Benz

Page 3, below right: © 2006 Mercedes-Benz

Page 4, above left and right: © 2010 Mercedes-Benz

Page 5, above left and right: courtesy of Williams Racing

Page 5, centre right: © Sutton Images / Getty Images

Page 5, below left: © dpa picture alliance / Alamy.com

Page 7: © Monaco Sports Group SAM

Page 8, above left: © 1 September 2024 Kym Illman

Page 8, above right: © 05/12/2021 Mercedes-Benz GP Ltd.

Page 8, centre left and right, below right: F1® images © Formula One World Championship Limited 2025

Page 8, below left: © Independent Photo Agency / Alamy.com

RAISING READERS
Books Build Bright Futures

Dear Reader,

We'd love your attention for one more page to tell you about the crisis in children's reading, and what we can all do.

Studies have shown that reading for fun is the **single biggest predictor of a child's future life chances** – more than family circumstance, parents' educational background or income. It improves academic results, mental health, wealth, communication skills, ambition and happiness.[1]

The number of children reading for fun is in rapid decline. Young people have a lot of competition for their time. In 2024, 1 in 10 children and young people in the UK aged 5 to 18 did not own a single book at home.[2]

Hachette works extensively with schools, libraries and literacy charities, but here are some ways we can all raise more readers:

- Reading to children for just 10 minutes a day makes a difference
- Don't give up if children aren't regular readers – there will be books for them!
- Visit bookshops and libraries to get recommendations
- Encourage them to listen to audiobooks
- Support school libraries
- Give books as gifts

There's a lot more information about how to encourage children to read on our website: **www.RaisingReaders.co.uk**

Thank you for reading.

hachette
UK

---

[1] OECD, '21st-Century Readers: Developing Literacy Skills in a Digital World', 2021, https://www.oecd.org/en/publications/21st-century-readers_a83d84cb-en.html

[2] National Literacy Trust, 'Book Ownership in 2024', November 2024, https://literacytrust.org.uk/research-services/research-reports/book-ownership-in-2024